Poststructuralism: A Very Short Introduction

VERY SHORT INTRODUCTIONS are for anyone wanting a stimulating and accessible way into a new subject. They are written by experts, and have been translated into more than 45 different languages.

The series began in 1995, and now covers a wide variety of topics in every discipline. The VSI library currently contains over 700 volumes—a Very Short Introduction to everything from Psychology and Philosophy of Science to American History and Relativity—and continues to grow in every subject area.

Very Short Introductions available now:

ABOLITIONISM Richard S. Newman
THE ABRAHAMIC RELIGIONS
  Charles L. Cohen
ACCOUNTING Christopher Nobes
ADOLESCENCE Peter K. Smith
THEODOR W. ADORNO
  Andrew Bowie
ADVERTISING Winston Fletcher
AERIAL WARFARE Frank Ledwidge
AESTHETICS Bence Nanay
AFRICAN AMERICAN RELIGION
  Eddie S. Glaude Jr
AFRICAN HISTORY John Parker and
  Richard Rathbone
AFRICAN POLITICS
  Ian Taylor
AFRICAN RELIGIONS
  Jacob K. Olupona
AGEING Nancy A. Pachana
AGNOSTICISM Robin Le Poidevin
AGRICULTURE Paul Brassley and
  Richard Soffe
ALEXANDER THE GREAT
  Hugh Bowden
ALGEBRA Peter M. Higgins
AMERICAN BUSINESS HISTORY
  Walter A. Friedman
AMERICAN CULTURAL HISTORY
  Eric Avila
AMERICAN FOREIGN RELATIONS
  Andrew Preston
AMERICAN HISTORY Paul S. Boyer
AMERICAN IMMIGRATION
  David A. Gerber

AMERICAN INTELLECTUAL
    HISTORY
  Jennifer Ratner-Rosenhagen
AMERICAN LEGAL HISTORY
  G. Edward White
AMERICAN MILITARY HISTORY
  Joseph T. Glatthaar
AMERICAN NAVAL HISTORY
  Craig L. Symonds
AMERICAN POETRY David Caplan
AMERICAN POLITICAL
    HISTORY Donald Critchlow
AMERICAN POLITICAL PARTIES
    AND ELECTIONS L. Sandy Maisel
AMERICAN POLITICS
  Richard M. Valelly
THE AMERICAN PRESIDENCY
  Charles O. Jones
THE AMERICAN REVOLUTION
  Robert J. Allison
AMERICAN SLAVERY
  Heather Andrea Williams
THE AMERICAN SOUTH
  Charles Reagan Wilson
THE AMERICAN WEST Stephen Aron
AMERICAN WOMEN'S HISTORY
  Susan Ware
AMPHIBIANS T. S. Kemp
ANAESTHESIA Aidan O'Donnell
ANALYTIC PHILOSOPHY
  Michael Beaney
ANARCHISM Colin Ward
ANCIENT ASSYRIA Karen Radner
ANCIENT EGYPT Ian Shaw

Available soon:

For more information visit our website

www.oup.com/vsi/

Catherine Belsey

POSTSTRUCTURALISM

A Very Short Introduction
SECOND EDITION

OXFORD
UNIVERSITY PRESS

OXFORD
UNIVERSITY PRESS

Great Clarendon Street, Oxford, OX2 6DP,
United Kingdom

Oxford University Press is a department of the University of Oxford.
It furthers the University's objective of excellence in research, scholarship,
and education by publishing worldwide. Oxford is a registered trade mark of
Oxford University Press in the UK and in certain other countries

First edition published 2002
This edition published 2022

Impression: 1

Published in the United States of America by Oxford University Press
198 Madison Avenue, New York, NY 10016, United States of America

British Library Cataloguing in Publication Data
Data available

Library of Congress Control Number: 2022934362

ISBN 978-0-19-885996-3

Printed in the UK by
Ashford Colour Press Ltd, Gosport, Hampshire

Contents

Foreword

Catherine Belsey was making her final alterations to this second edition of *Poststructuralism: A Very Short Introduction* in October 2020 when she suffered a stroke at home in Cambridge. She spent the next few months in hospital before being moved to a hospice, where she died on the morning of 14 February 2021.

Eighteen months earlier, Kate asked me out of the blue if I would oversee her literary affairs following her death. I protested that an immortal had no need of such an earthly arrangement, but she took from my hands the copy of *Tales of the Troubled Dead* with which she had just presented me. Retrieving a pen from her handbag, she wrote a message inside the cover of the book: 'For Neil, my literary executor—for the record—from Kate.' She assured me that she would haunt me if I didn't do my job properly.

For the record, I finalized the present text for publication at the request of Kate's family, using two sources: a file from Kate's computer and a typescript with handwritten annotations that was found on her desk. 'I know that I can no longer reach her', writes Joan Didion towards the end of *Blue Nights*, her memoir about the death of her daughter. I knew—obviously, painfully, daily—that I could no longer reach Kate while I was settling her sentences for print, so I turned at times for advice to Julia Thomas, Irene Morra, Laurence Totelin, Kim Gilchrist, and Becky Munford. Kate's words

can now reach their readers in the form, I believe, that she desired.
I hope that she has no need to haunt me.

Neil Badmington,
Cardiff, July 2021

List of illustrations

Chapter 1
Creatures of difference

When Lewis Carroll's Humpty Dumpty discusses the question of meaning with Alice, which one of them is right?

In *Through the Looking Glass* Humpty Dumpty engages Alice in one argument after another, just as if dialogue were a competition (see Figure 1). Having demonstrated to his own satisfaction, if not Alice's, that unbirthday presents are to be preferred because people can have them more often, he adds triumphantly, 'There's glory for you!'

Torn between the desire to placate him and good common sense, Alice rejoins, 'I don't know what you mean by "glory".' So Humpty Dumpty explains:

> 'I meant "there's a nice knock-down argument for you!"'
> 'But "glory" doesn't mean "a nice knock-down argument",' Alice objected.
> 'When I use a word,' Humpty Dumpty said in a rather scornful tone, 'it means just what I choose it to mean—neither more nor less.'
> 'The question is,' said Alice, 'whether you can make words mean so many different things.'
> 'The question is,' said Humpty Dumpty, 'which is to be Master—that's all.'

1. Alice and Humpty Dumpty. Which of them is right?

Alice's scepticism is surely justified? Meaning is not at our disposal, or we could never communicate with others. We learn our native language and, in the process, internalize the meanings other people exchange. Small children find out from those who already know how to distinguish ducks from squirrels: ducks are the ones that fly. And children make mistakes: aeroplanes fly, but they are not ducks. Glory is not a nice knock-down argument.

Language makes conversation possible, but only to the degree that we use it appropriately, reproducing the meanings already in circulation. As this dialogue demonstrates, there is no such thing as a private language. Humpty Dumpty has to 'translate' his before he can communicate with Alice.

Language and knowledge

Understood in the broad sense of the term to embrace all signifying systems, including images and symbols, language gives us access to information. Command of a new knowledge very often amounts to learning the appropriate use of a new vocabulary and syntax. To the extent that people understand economics, they demonstrate the fact by using its terms and arranging them in an appropriate order. A grasp of psychoanalysis means the ability to exchange words like 'unconscious', 'repression', or 'transference'. Mathematics, science, and logic have their own symbolic systems, and qualified practitioners are those who know how to inhabit them. The examination system is above all a way of policing the profession, making sure that those who qualify to join it know how its language or symbols are conventionally deployed.

Film directors and advertisers, meanwhile, know the meanings conveyed by pictures of cute children or sleek kitchens. Language in this broad sense is also a source of social values. In learning to use words like 'democracy' and 'dictatorship' appropriately, for instance, Western children learn about political systems, but they also absorb as they do so the value their culture invests in these respective forms of government. For better or worse, Western children learn early on, without having to be explicitly taught, that dictatorship is oppressive and democracy so precious that it is worth fighting for. In many cultures, the flag is the visual indicator of a national identity that must be defended—by force, if necessary.

Language and cultural change

If language, broadly understood, transmits the knowledges and values that constitute a culture, it follows that the existing meanings are not ours to command. And yet is it possible that the disdainful Humpty Dumpty has a point after all? To reproduce existing meanings exactly is also to reaffirm the knowledges our culture takes for granted, and the values that precede us—the norms, therefore, of the previous generation. Examination papers in economics, mathematics, or media studies are set and marked by existing practitioners, experts in the field, whose job it is to mark down misunderstandings and misuses of the conventional vocabulary.

In that respect, meanings exercise a degree of control when they inculcate obedience to the discipline inscribed in them. And this is by no means purely institutional, or confined to the educational process. A generation ago campaigners for women's rights recognized (not for the first time) the degree to which 'woman' meant domesticity, nurturing, dependence, and the ways in which anti-feminist jokes, for instance, reproduced the stereotypes of the helpless little girl or the ageing harridan. The question feminists confronted was precisely who was to be Master, as Humpty Dumpty puts it.

In this particular case, however, his formulation was self-evidently not one we could adopt. The term 'Master' would hardly help the feminist cause, but 'Mistress' would not easily take its place, since it carried sexual connotations that detracted from the authority we were looking for. The right word in a new situation does not always readily present itself. Language sometimes seems to lead a life of its own. Words are unruly: 'They've a temper, some of them,' Humpty Dumpty goes on to observe.

In this case the masculine and feminine values were not symmetrical—and nor, of course, was the culture. Without

4

supposing this was the only change necessary, we set out to modify the language, annoying conservatives with coinages like 'spokesperson' and 's/he'. We refused to laugh at misogyny, and ignored the taunts that we had no sense of humour.

Campaigners against racism, too, know that dialogue can become the kind of competition Humpty Dumpty's words parodied. Perhaps in a way it always is. We rightly reproach our politicians when their chosen vocabulary inflames existing conflicts.

Language is not in any sense personal or private. But it offers options and individuals can alter it, as long as others adopt their changes. What, after all, do great poets, philosophers, and scientists do, but change our vocabulary? Shakespeare invented hundreds of words. Developing disciplines do the same. In the course of the 20th century, science progressively named 'electrons', 'protons', 'neutrons', and 'quarks', not to mention dark matter and black holes. A new pandemic appears and, in no time, native speakers of English find themselves discussing 'social distancing' and 'self-isolation', as well as Covid-19.

Poststructuralism is difficult to the extent that its practitioners use old words in unfamiliar ways, or fresh terms to say what cannot be said otherwise. This novel vocabulary still elicits some resistance, but the issue we confront is how far we should let the existing language impose limits on what it is possible to think.

Poststructuralism and language

Poststructuralism groups a number of disparate theories concerning the relationship between human beings, the world, and the practice of making, reproducing, and challenging meanings. While these speculations differ from one another in important respects, they begin from certain common assumptions. On the one hand, poststructuralists affirm, consciousness is not the origin of the language we speak and the images we recognize, so much as the product of the meanings we learn and reproduce. On the other hand, communication changes all the time, with or without intervention from us, and we can choose to intervene with a view to altering the meanings—which is to say the norms and values—our culture takes for granted. The question is the one Humpty Dumpty poses: who is to be in control?

This very short introduction will trace some of the arguments that have led poststructuralists to question traditional theories of language and culture, and with them customary accounts of what it is possible to know, as well as what it is to be a human being. Poststructuralism offers a range of ways to consider our place in the world that compete with conventional explanations.

The importance of language

Most of the time the language we speak is barely visible to us. We are more concerned with what it can do: describe our symptoms; induce the neighbours to keep the noise down; get us off the hook when we've done something bad. And yet few issues are more important in human life. After the food and shelter that are necessary to survival, language and its visual analogues exercise the most crucial determinations in our social relations, our thought processes, and our understanding of who and what we are.

Even food and shelter themselves do not come into our lives undefined. Menus that offer 'luscious, slow-roasted aubergine, infused with zingy tamarind sauce' may take this principle to extremes, but for me, I remember, 'scrag end stew' was a lost cause from the beginning.

Houses, too, are characterized in language, and not only by estate agents. We might want to live in one we could justifiably call old or quaint, modern or minimalist, but might feel less enthusiastic once we had thought of it as decrepit, poky, brash, or bleak. Paint manufacturers know that we are more likely to coat our walls in a colour marketed as 'Morning Sun' than one called 'Custard', even if the pigmentation is exactly the same.

In this sense language intervenes between human beings and their world. A party game involves blindfolding one player as a prelude to guessing what foods are placed on his or her tongue. Whether consciously or not, guessing means classifying in accordance with the system of differences the language already provides: is it sweet or savoury? hot or cold? bland or bitter?

Poststructuralists share the view that the distinctions we make are not necessarily given by the world around us, but are instead produced by the symbolic systems we learn. How else would we know the difference between pixies and gnomes, or March Hares, Cheshire Cats, and talking eggs? But we learn our native tongue at such an early age that it seems transparent, a window onto a world of things, even if some of those things are in practice imaginary, no more than ideas of things, derived from children's stories.

Are ideas the source of meaning, then? That was once the conventional view, but our ideas are not, poststructuralists believe, the origin of the language we speak. Indeed, the reverse is the case. Ideas are the effect of the meanings we learn and reproduce. We learned our idea of Humpty Dumpty (if we did) from nursery rhymes, Lewis Carroll, and John Tenniel, who illustrated the *Alice* books. In its account of how we become meaning animals, and the role meaning plays in our understanding of the world, poststructuralism represents a modern challenge to traditional beliefs.

Meaning

What is meaning? Where do meanings came from? Perhaps the question finds more focus in relation to a specific instance. What, then, does the word 'modern' mean in the sentence at the end of the last section? What precise timespan does 'modern' cover?

The answer seems to vary with the context. As a description of the poststructuralist resistance to inherited convictions, it may mean nothing much more specific than 'new'. Modern history, on the other hand, generally concerns the period since the 17th century. And yet we think of modern languages as distinct from Latin and Greek, while modern furniture almost certainly belongs to the 20th century or later. In these instances 'modern' defines no common chronological period: modern history belongs to about the last 400 years, modern languages to perhaps the last thousand, and modern furniture to no more than the last hundred or so. The modern challenge of poststructuralism itself is a product of roughly the last half-century.

The term 'modern', in other words, has no positive content, but owes its meaning to difference. What is modern is in these instances respectively 'not medieval', 'not ancient', 'not antique', or simply 'not traditional'. But at least in all these cases 'modern' distinguishes a period that is more recent than another. Modern*ism*, however, denoting a style in art and literature, and associated with the first half of the 20th century, is probably no longer the latest thing, while in the compound 'postmodern', sometimes used to define our own era, modernity has explicitly become, paradoxically, a thing of the past.

Nevertheless, although it seems to refer to no constant period, we are usually able to understand and use the word 'modern' without difficulty. How? In the *Course in General Linguistics*, first published in 1916, the Swiss linguist Ferdinand de Saussure proposed that 'in language there are only differences *without positive terms*', and this observation initiated a train of thought that would be taken up by a succession of figures in a range of disciplines during the course of the following century. Poststructuralism begins from Saussure's account of how we are able to exchange meanings, and goes on to conceive of human beings as animals possessing this capability to an exceptional degree. Insofar as language is formative, we are creatures of difference.

In the book that did most to provide a starting point for the theories that will be our concern, Saussure proposed that meaning did not depend on reference to the world, or even to ideas. On the contrary. He argued that, if the things or concepts language named already existed outside it, words would have exact equivalents from one language to another, and translation would be easy. But as all translators know, nothing could be further from the case. *'Toto, sois sage,'* we dutifully intoned in my French class when I was 11, 'Toto, be good.' But even at that early stage we sensed that *sage* and 'good' were not always interchangeable. 'A good time' in French, we knew, would not be *sage* at all, since the term implied sense or wisdom. We were, in addition, using a mode of address that had no English translation. The second person singular that exists in so many European languages (*tu, Du*) can cause native speakers of English embarrassment when we try to communicate in other tongues, since it carries values of intimacy or hierarchy which may give offence in the wrong places.

Genders and tenses do not necessarily correspond from one language to another. The morning is masculine in French (*le matin*), feminine in Italian (*la mattina*). French has the past historic, a special tense for telling stories. Some languages have more than one plural form. Differences that are given in one language have to be mastered, often with difficulty, by those whose mother tongue divides up the world in another way.

We are compelled to conclude either that some languages misrepresent the way things are, while our own describes the world accurately, or that language, which seems to name units given in nature, does not in practice depend on reference to things, or even to our ideas of things. Instead, the units that seem to exist so unproblematically may be differentiated from one another by language itself, so that we think of them as natural, just as we may perceive the continuous spectrum of the rainbow in terms of seven distinct colours.

A century ago many European nations were ready to impose their own classifications on other cultures, where imperial conquest made this possible. But the multicultural societies that have resulted from the decline of empire are willing to be more generous in their recognition of other accounts of the world, which is to say, other networks of differences.

A mother tongue represents a way of understanding the world, of differentiating between things and relating them to one another. Culture is inscribed in language. The Kenyan writer Ngugi wa Thiong'o wrote his first works of fiction in English. Later, it came to seem to him that this practice conceded too much to the influence of the former colonial power, and the continued economic and cultural neo-colonialism of the West. However African the content and themes of his early novels, the novel itself was a European genre, its structure reproducing a Western pattern of thought. Moreover, the English language could not do justice to Kenyan perceptions of the world. He then began to write in Gikuyu, drawing on indigenous forms of narrative and drama.

Difference, not reference

People fluent in more than one language tend to agree that each tongue offers a distinctive take on things. The simple inference that meaning is differential, not referential, has profound implications for our understanding of the relations between human beings and the world. Poststructuralism evolved as Saussure's account of meaning was taken up by later generations, especially in France when, after the Second World War, the history of Nazism—and of collaboration with it in occupied France— seemed to demand an explanation that existing theories of culture were unable to provide. The key term in the development of poststructuralism is Saussure's 'difference'.

Saussure and the sign

Traditionally, words had been thought of as signs. The sign seemed to represent (re-present) a presence that existed elsewhere, to stand as the sign *of* something. In everyday English we still refer to the meaning 'behind' the words, as if meaning existed somewhere on the other side of speech or writing. Saussure's work changed that. For him meaning resides in the sign and nowhere else.

In order to make the point clear, he divided the sign in two: on the one hand, the signifier, the sound or the visual appearance of the word, phrase, or image in question; on the other, the signified, its meaning. In ordinary circumstances the distinction is purely methodological. We rarely see a signifier which does not signify, or mean something. But an unknown language consists entirely of signifiers in isolation. We hear sounds and assume that they signify, since we see native speakers apparently conversing, but to us they mean nothing. Or we see a page of impenetrable written characters. Ancient artefacts unearthed in the 1890s at Knossos on Crete bore Minoan writings that no one at the time could read. In the 1950s, the latest script, known as Linear B, was deciphered, invested with meaning. But Linear A still consists mainly of signifiers that no longer signify to us (see Figure 2).

If you don't happen to know Greek, this is a pure signifier:

λόγος

In its written form it makes this shape; spoken aloud, it makes a particular sound: logos. And if you do know Greek, it brings with it a signified that has no exact equivalent in English, but ranges between 'word', 'account', 'meaning', and 'thought'. Changing the

11

2. Ancient signifiers that mostly no longer signify.

shape very slightly—and silently—by capitalizing the initial letter, we turn it into Λόγος and the signified changes to something like 'God' or 'Reason'.

Neither element of the sign determines the other: the signifier does not 'express' the meaning, nor does the signified 'resemble' the form or sound. On the contrary, the relationship between signifier and signified is arbitrary. There is nothing doggy about the word 'dog'. There can't be, since the French recognize much the same characteristics in *un chien*. Even in languages with a shared European history, *Schwein, maiale, porc,* and *pig* have more or less the same signified. Children learn to distinguish the

Signifiers

Q. Why use the jargon term, 'signifier'? Why not just say 'word'?

A. Because words are not the only signifiers. Traffic lights, arrows, and crossing indicators signify. So do gestures: pointing, shaking hands, punching the air. Yawns, gasps, and screams are all signifiers—in the sense that they may be interpreted by those around us, even if that was not what we intended. Paintings signify. Sometimes a group of words constitutes one signifier: 'How are you?' is not most usefully broken down into its component words; rather, it represents a single greeting, registers an interest—and probably *doesn't* in practice invite a list of symptoms, except in the doctor's surgery.

meaning when they learn the signifier. To use a term appropriately is to know what it means.

Grown-ups go on learning new signifiers, and the process is nowhere clearer than in the realm of ideas. Most people do not have the idea of poststructuralism first, and then go on to discover the name. Instead, now that the term exists, we learn how to use it appropriately in the course of internalizing its meaning. 'Whether we take the signified or the signifier', Saussure argues, 'language has neither ideas nor sounds that existed before the linguistic system, but only conceptual and phonic differences that have issued from the system.'

René Magritte's word-paintings wittily exploit the arbitrariness of the relationship between the signifier and meaning. Children used to learn to read from primers that showed pictures of things with their names underneath, to teach them what the written signifier meant. Magritte's *The Key to Dreams* (1935) shows four such pictures, but only the last, 'the valise', is appropriately labelled (see Figure 3).

Ferdinand de Saussure, 1857–1913

Professor of Linguistics in Paris, he moved to the University of Geneva in 1906, where he began to give the lectures that would constitute the *Course in General Linguistics* (1916). Dissatisfied with the conventional historical (diachronic) character of the discipline, Saussure chose to analyse the workings of language in its existing (synchronic) form. If objects or ideas were knowable outside the signifiers that distinguished them from each other, Saussure argued, terms would have exact equivalents from one language to another, but since translation is so often a quest for approximations, meaning must depend on difference, not on reference to things or concepts. The *Course* was put together by his students after his death. Ironically, one of the figures who exerted the most influence on what would evolve as poststructuralism was thus not in the conventional sense the author of his own book.

Suppose 'bird' really signified 'jug'. What difference would it make? Any, or none? Magritte places his misnamed objects against what the frame indicates are window panes. But these panes are painted black; the window is opaque; it does not allow us to see a world of things on the other side of it. Both name and object are on the same side of the glass, if glass it is. Here language is not a window onto the world.

Or perhaps, instead, Magritte's window should be seen as a blackboard, traditional source of instruction about the world, where the words are chalked below the images? If so, it is surely an ironic one: the children in this class are being grossly misled. While it parodies a reading lesson, does *The Key to Dreams* also offer a sideways glance at Sigmund Freud's *Interpretation of Dreams*? The French titles of the painting and the book differ but

14

3. René Magritte's *The Key to Dreams* parodies a reading primer. Is it also a visual-verbal 'poem'?

Freud's work promises to unlock unexpected meanings for the objects that appear in sleep.

But then again, is there irony here at all? Common sense would say so, but common sense did not do justice to Humpty Dumpty, who turned out to have a point, however improbably. Perhaps *The Key to Dreams* treats its words and images as two kinds of signifiers, one textual, the other pictorial? Isolated visual signifiers are familiar to us, after all, in the form of road signs or brand logos. What are paintings themselves, but assemblages of visual signifiers?

If we read the picture that way, we could create our own connections between the sets of signifiers in Magritte's painting. Is there an unforeseen parallel between time and the wind, both in flight, both imperceptible? Or could this door, half-enclosing a wistful horse, be a stable door? Is there an untold story here? The painting does not answer either question; instead, it keeps its options open or, in poststructuralist terms, doesn't close down on a final signified.

The primacy of the signifier

Poetry, too, works by proposing parallels, inviting the reader to make unexpected connections between apparently distinct signifiers. Amy Lowell's Imagist poem 'Wind and Silver' draws an analogy that depends on the conjunction of unpredictability with visual appropriateness:

Greatly shining,
The Autumn moon floats in the thin sky;
And the fish-ponds shake their backs and flash their dragon scales
As she passes over them.

And yet, you might object, this moon and these fish-ponds are more than signifiers. Surely they exist, as things? We 'see' their referents in their absence, in our mind's eye, and that is the source of any pleasure we derive from the poem.

Yes, in a way. But what the poem does is isolate these images from the 'noise' that would surround them in actuality, pausing them for contemplation. The signifier condenses and separates off the comparison it creates from the distinct experience as it might exist in a world of reference, and in the process generates an association—the ethereal effect of the extra-bright harvest moon moving above water—that surely relegates the ponds themselves to the very edges of our interest. The uncanny impression depends (of course) on differences—between night and day, the heavens and the earth—brought into question, as the strange light transforms the mundane. There is nothing referential about a sky described as 'thin' or pools of water rendered as creatures from an ancient mythology stirred into vivid life.

That haunting quality is also an effect of the fact that we read these words as poetry: the four lines isolated on the white space of the page; the sound patterns made up of successive monosyllables, and the near-rhymes, 'shining' and 'sky', 'shake' and 'scales', 'backs' and 'flash'. Rhythm plays its part too, the two short lines enclosing the long ones, the longest alone devoted to the surprise transformation of the ponds. While the modernist poem breaks with traditional English metres, its own smooth flow, anything but prosaic, owes a debt to Japanese haiku.

Julia Kristeva calls this signifying capability that is not derived from the meanings of the words 'the semiotic'. It evokes, she maintains, the sound produced by the rhythmic babbling of small children who cannot yet speak. The semiotic exists prior to the acquisition of meaning. Such sound effects, as they reappear in poetry, are musical, patterned; they disrupt the purely 'thetic' (thesis-making) logic of rational argument by drawing on a sense or sensation that Kristeva identifies as either supplementing or conflicting with surface meaning.

'The Death of the Author'

How would we expect to confirm our reading of Lowell's poem or Magritte's picture? Traditional criticism would say we should ask the author, and if the author is dead, as in these cases, we should read biographies, diaries, or letters, until we can guess what the author might have intended. Poststructuralism, however, disagrees. If signifying practices are not ours to possess, but are learnt, modified, and shared, ideas are their effect rather than their cause. And if poems and paintings rely on or challenge convention, their meanings may well exceed the artist's intention. In that case, there is no final answer to the question of what any example of signifying practice ultimately means.

That does not imply, on the other hand, that it means whatever we like. Humpty Dumpty is wrong to think that language is entirely subject to our whim. A purely private language does not permit dialogue, and so hardly qualifies as a *language* at all. But a specific instance of signifying practice can mean whatever the public and shared possibilities of these signifiers in this order will permit.

Roland Barthes, 1915–80

Professor of Literary Semiology (a title he chose himself) at the Collège de France. The work that made him famous was *Mythologies*, published in French in 1957 (see Chapter 2) but his most influential work of literary criticism was *S/Z* (1970), a brilliant close analysis of a Balzac story that turns out to be much more complex—and more interesting—than a casual reading might suggest. His writing is always dazzling: witty, stylish, apparently mischievous and yet persuasive, serious in its implications, for all the extravagance of the manner. Among the most pleasurable of his books, *A Lover's Discourse: Fragments* (1977) offers a series of brief dramatic monologues demonstrating the pains and pleasures—as well as the derivative character—of the state of being in love. Even this most individual and personal of conditions, the book indicates, is 'citational', learnt from the love stories we have read, or seen at the movies. 'Every other night, on TV', it points out, 'someone says: *I love you.*'

In 1968, a year of insurrection and manifestos, when the Renault workers and the students took temporary control of the streets of Paris, Roland Barthes coincidentally proclaimed in France what he called 'The Death of the Author'. His argument depends on the fact that the first-person signifier *I* is a 'shifter': it moves from speaker to speaker as each lays claim to it. In linguistic terms, the author is never more than the figure produced by the use of *I*, just as we constitute ourselves subjects of the sentences we speak by the same means. If I say, 'I am hungry', I may be all sorts of other things too, but as far as the meaning of my words is concerned, I am no more at that moment than a person claiming to be hungry. 'Linguistically, the author is never more than the instance writing,' Barthes insists.

Citationality

How, then, do works of art signify? By their difference, of course! It is not only at the level of the individual word, phrase, or image that meaning depends on difference. Magritte's painting alludes to old-fashioned school primers, and crucially differs from them; possibly, it invokes—and parodies—Freud. To see what is being 'cited' in the picture is to grasp part of what we call the 'point', which is to say, the meaning.

Moreover, *The Key to Dreams* also alludes to a long tradition of Western painting, invoking the conventions of Renaissance realism in its convincing depiction of individual objects, but locating itself as modernist by putting them in unlikely places. Imagist poems depend for their meaning not only on the combinations of individual words that compose them but also on their difference from the lyric tradition, isolating a fragmentary and instantaneous impression without reference to a context, a speaker, or a state of mind.

The Author

Q. What did Barthes have against authors? Did he think books wrote themselves?

A. He was not concerned about the author, so much as the Author. His real target was the critical institution, which maintains its control over the meaning of literary texts by making knowledge of the author's life and times the key to the only possible reading. The Author is then brought in as the explanation of the work, the final signified, closing down the possibility of new interpretations based on attention to the signifiers themselves—such characteristics of the text as genre, allusions to other texts, or surprising breaks with expectation.

We should not, therefore, try to get 'behind' the work, Barthes argues, to the author or artist. Instead, 'the space of writing is to be ranged over, not pierced' (and the metaphor suggests that the quest for intention generates a kind of violence). We should look *at* the text, Barthes urges, not through it. And his manifesto concludes with a ringing declaration: 'the birth of the reader must be at the cost of the death of the Author'.

The reader

Roland Barthes wants us to read the text, not something else that we imagine would provide a clue to it, or a confirmation of our interpretation. But he is not arguing for subjectivism, the view that the text's associations for me personally, whatever they might happen to be, will do as an account of its meaning. Instead, his reader is not an individual, not a real person at all, but 'the space on which all the quotations that make up a writing are inscribed without any of them being lost'. Such a 'space' does not exist, except as an ideal type, a timeless, utopian, model reader. In practice, some of us will see some of the possibilities, some others, and the text itself refuses to say which is 'right'. Indeed, it becomes unclear just what 'right' would mean, though it's still possible, if we don't know the words, or we don't pay sufficient attention to them, or miss a citation, or mistake the genre, to be wrong. If I read Amy Lowell's poem as a shopping list, I'd be out of order.

Popular usage

Is poststructuralism only concerned with art and literature, then? A new way of approaching high culture? Not at all. Any arrangement of signifiers, it proposes, can be treated as undecidable in the same kind of way. Even the simplest instances of signification may do more work than we necessarily realize. I grew up in a world of posters which affirmed in large letters, 'Guinness is good for you!' Since I was too young to like beer in those days, I didn't give them much thought. Now, however, I wonder just what was being claimed here.

It's true that stout was held to be full of nutritional value, and was often treated as a health drink, especially by middle-aged women. And Guinness was stout. But is that the whole story? The posters also showed comic cartoon animals in bright colours. Weren't these visual signifiers associating the drink with pleasure, laughter, the exchange of jokes? Weren't the adverts indicating that enjoying yourself was 'good for you', taking you out of yourself, as we might once have said? And was it the sociability of the pub, or the alcohol, that would make you see the world in the bright primary colours of the posters themselves? Either way, the claim of the images, or the words and the images taken together, was that Guinness was 'good for' your world picture, brightening the way things looked. The advertisers, I now think, were exploiting the plurality of the signifier, withholding the gratification (or do I really mean the banality?) of a final signified.

If so, the simplicity of the slogan is as deceptive as the apparent straightforwardness of Balzac's story. And in advertising, as in art, reading produces an interpretation that has no final guarantees elsewhere. There is more to be said in the next chapter about images of the world as it appears in everyday representation.

Chapter 2
Difference and culture

'Daz drives out stains.' What links 1950s washing powders with international politics? Traditional domestic cleaning products that used bleach or ammonia 'killed' germs. By contrast, what was new in the imagery of household detergents, available for the first time just after the Second World War, was that they separated dirt from the fabric decisively but without 'violence'. 'Their ideal role is to liberate the object from its circumstantial imperfection,' Roland Barthes proposes, expelling the enemy of whiteness as it submits to the superior virtue of washing powder. 'Their function is keeping public order not making war.'

Adverts for skincare products, he argues, are 'similarly based on a kind of epic representation of the intimate', but here the moisturizers 'penetrate' the skin from outside, 'infiltrate' deep layers, and subvert its propensity to wrinkle.

Though Barthes does not explicitly say so, the implication is that these ads make their case by citing the imagery of the Cold War. In post-war politics, violence gave way to a conflict based on espionage and infiltration. Undercover agents would keep order by unmasking the left at home. Abroad, spies would destabilize communist states, inciting their own citizens to effect their own liberation by driving out the enemies of capitalism. Drawing on the imagery of this struggle, publicity for products that had no apparent connection with it could count on unconscious consumer recognition of the values it reaffirmed.

These days, many advertisers have read *Mythologies*, first published in French as a book in 1957. Here Barthes explores the implications of Saussure's account of language for our understanding of Western culture. In the *Course in General Linguistics* Saussure had argued:

> *A science that studies the life of signs within society is conceivable*...I shall call it *semiology* (from Greek *semeion* 'sign').....Linguistics is only a part of the general science of semiology...By studying rites, customs, etc. as signs, I believe that we shall throw new light on the facts and point up the need for including them in a science of semiology.

We probably need not take the term 'science' too literally here. In the early years of the 20th century, when Saussure was giving the lectures that would become the *Course*, science was highly valued. Any new knowledge worth its salt claimed to be a science. (At the same historical moment Freud was making identical claims for his fledgling psychoanalysis.) In any case, *science* in French tends to mean any exact or methodical knowledge, including what English speakers think of as scientific knowledge, but not confined to it.

Although *Mythologies* concludes with an essay that self-consciously sets out to develop Saussure's account of the discipline of semiology (or semiotics: the two have become virtually interchangeable), the real pleasure and interest of the book lies in its anything but scientific readings of cultural concerns from striptease to children's toys, from 'The Face of Garbo' to 'The Brain of Einstein'. These short pieces, originally published as journalism, set out to expose what was at stake in the representation of the everyday.

Presumably, even in 1957 most people knew that advertising was designed to sell them commodities, but what was not so immediately apparent was the citationality of this process, including the marketing of soap powders and skin creams, consciously or unconsciously, in the vocabulary of international relations. Today, when we are more alert to the way the everyday is presented to us, the teaching of media studies probably owes to Roland Barthes both its awareness of the subtlety of the signifying practices involved and its recognition that the inscription of a point of view does not have to be thought out or deliberate.

Values

Barthes's comments were not confined to advertisements or, indeed, to news and public events. The commonplace, Saussure's 'rites, customs, etc.', can be just as revealing. What we take for granted can tell us as much about our values as the opinions we deliberately arrive at after thought and discussion. Why do travel guides celebrate undulating scenery as picturesque? A possible answer: puritanism promotes clean air and hard work. 'Only mountains, gorges, defiles and torrents can have access to the pantheon of travel, inasmuch, probably, as they seem to encourage a morality of effort and solitude.'

Sometimes, the devil is in the detail. Joseph L. Mankiewicz's film of *Julius Caesar* (1953) shows all the men with their hair combed forward to indicate Roman-ness. The men also sweat a good deal. This, *Mythologies* goes on to argue, signifies *thinking* (about politics). Western values are so anti-intellectual that, by the repeated rejection of new ideas in the name of common sense, 'laziness is promoted to the rank of rigour'. Such a world sees thought as a process unnatural enough to cause perspiration.

It's outrageous, of course. But, even in translation, the wit and fluency of the essays are likely to enlist a certain complicity on the part of the reader. Besides, it is always gratifying to have the sense that we see 'through' the masks and masquerades of our own culture.

On the other hand, we should perhaps beware of that 'through': there may be more meaning *in* the everyday than meets the eye but, if Saussure is right about the non-referential character of language, there are no ideas or values motivating it from outside or beyond culture itself. Culture consists of the meanings its subjects produce and reproduce. Even in the process of analysing it, we are simply taking up another position in culture, inhabiting a space culture itself provides, or can be induced to provide.

Your turn

Semiology (or semiotics) sounds easy enough, doesn't it? So do you want to try?

The passage that follows is from the first page of George Eliot's *Adam Bede*. No prior knowledge of literary criticism is required: you are a semiologist, looking for the cultural values that are affirmed or re-affirmed in the text. And remember that, to be true to Barthes, you should ignore any information you have about the author. Intention is not the issue. It might help, though, to know that, although the story begins at the end of the 18th century, the novel was first published in 1859, directly after its completion 60 years later. So look out for nostalgia. And beware of the dog.

> I will show you the roomy workshop of Mr Jonathan Burge, carpenter and builder in the village of Hayslope, as it appeared on the eighteenth of June, in the year of our Lord 1799.
>
> The afternoon sun was warm on the five workmen there, busy upon doors and window-frames and wainscoting. A scent of pine-wood from a tent-like pile of planks outside the open door mingled itself with the scent of the elder-bushes which were spreading their summer snow close to the open window opposite; the slanting sunbeams shone through the transparent shavings that flew before the steady plane, and lit up the fine grain of the oak panelling which stood propped against the wall. On a heap of those

soft shavings a rough grey shepherd-dog had made himself a
pleasant bed, and was lying with his nose between his fore-paws,
occasionally wrinkling his brows to cast a glance at the tallest of the
five workmen, who was carving a shield in the centre of a wooden
mantelpiece. It was to this workman that the strong baritone
belonged which was heard above the sound of the plane and
hammer singing—

> 'Awake, my soul, and with the sun
> Thy daily stage of duty run;
> Shake off dull sloth…'

As you almost certainly noticed, the passage endorses hard work.
This is an idealizing picture of unalienated labour. In a village
named to suggest a timeless landscape, untouched by the
industrial revolution's dark, satanic mills, the men sing as they
toil, in harmony with their world. The material they shape—
before the machines take over—is natural, and its scents become
continuous ('mingle') with the smells of uncultivated nature in the
open air. As the mantelpiece and panelling indicate, their project
is the improvement of a home: virtuous work serves domesticity,
family values.

The central figure is a skilled labourer: he is carving a coat of arms
for the gentry and he does not question the hierarchy this implies.
He is also the tallest of the men. Height is a consistent signifier of
authority in Western culture. The dog that occasionally glances at
him clearly recognizes its master. This is a serious, workman's dog,
not the Pekinese or poodle that would denote a fop, and it is both
relaxed and disciplined, which simultaneously demonstrates and
justifies its confidence in the order of things.

In English fiction, dogs *know*. And this passage links a
quintessential Englishness with nature in the name of the village
(Hayslope), the materials (oak and pine), and the insistent
ruralness of the scene. Evidence to the contrary notwithstanding,

England still *is* the countryside, we are to understand, and any threat to its conservation is a scandal because it threatens Englishness itself.

Nature v. history

What does this reading achieve? Does the interpretation we have produced here matter? And are the short essays that compose *Mythologies* any more than a stylish example of Gallic wit? Myths, Barthes proposes, show culture masquerading as natural, given, inevitable.

A cover of the magazine *Paris Match* showed a black soldier in French uniform saluting the flag. What did this signify? That France was a great empire, and that all her subjects, regardless of 'race', willingly acknowledged her right to co-opt their service, and indeed their lives, in her defence.

The photograph, Barthes affirms, natural-izes imperialism. Nineteenth-century realist fiction similarly natural-izes the class structure. *Adam Bede* shows a working man gladly and virtuously carving for someone else a family crest which denotes an entitlement to own land, while he needs to earn his living. However sympathetic or, indeed, heroic, they may be as individuals, the deserving poor have to work for the benefit of other people—naturally.

History offers any number of cases where the product of history is universalized as 'the human condition'. When the Berlin Wall came down in 1989, the West was convinced that nature, which is to say capitalism, had reasserted itself after the unnatural imposition of communism by force, against the will of the people. Television pictures of festive crowds confirmed this view. Many in the same crowds would in due course be surprised to find that everyday life in a capitalist regime was not quite as benign as Hollywood had led them to believe. In practice, their disillusionment with Soviet-style communism was not necessarily proof of the naturalness of the free market.

If myth converts history into nature, the task of the mythographer is to rediscover the element of history that motivates the myth, to elicit what is specific to a given time and place, asking what interests are served by the naturalization of particular convictions and values.

'Eternal Man'

In this respect, *Mythologies* indicates, our own historical moment is special. We have myths as never before. Why? Because the form of ownership that determines the nature of our society is bourgeois, Barthes says, and it is the particular property of bourgeois ideology to efface itself by passing for nature. There are no bourgeois thought-police; no one votes 'bourgeois'; the bourgeoisie simply spreads its values everywhere without naming itself as a class at all. The press, the judicial system, cookery books, and weddings are all silently and anonymously informed by the representation the bourgeoisie transmits of the relations between human beings and the world. This understanding of the way things are is so pervasive that it comes to seem like a law of nature, and its hero is 'Eternal Man', a classless but generally white and still often male figure, who recognizes his own ideals in the norms of good sense and good taste that prevail at any given time.

Marxism and ideology

At this point in the argument, as you may have noticed, *Mythologies* has adopted a vocabulary derived from Marxism. Barthes was not himself a Marxist, but it was impossible to be an intellectual in Paris in the post-war era without taking Marxism into account. Many of the influential theorists of the time defined their own positions in line with or against the views of the French Communist Party.

Marxism already offered an account of culture. Karl Marx and Friedrich Engels wrote *The German Ideology* in 1845–6, before the revolutions that occurred all over Europe in 1848. They did not publish this early work, which survived only in manuscript until the 1930s, but among all sorts of local observations, of interest now mainly to historians of ideas, the first part in particular includes a number of insights, not always fully worked out, but way in advance of their time.

'Ideology', Marx and Engels proposed, consists of the forms of social exchange that correspond to the mode of ownership prevailing at the time. They saw history as a succession of forms of possession, tribal in the first instance, then 'communal' in the city states of Greece and Rome, next feudal, and now capitalist. Ideology justifies the rule of each ruling class, whether as chieftains, patricians, landowners, or those with capital, the bourgeoisie. And in an example that perfectly anticipates semiology, Marx and Engels point out that under feudalism we hear a good deal about 'honour' and 'loyalty', but when capitalism takes over, 'freedom' and 'equality' (of opportunity, presumably) rapidly take their place.

Marxism

You may well ask if Marxism is completely discredited. Does anyone outside North Korea take it seriously, since Eastern Europe opted for capitalism and even China has embraced the market? Arguably, totalitarian regimes owe very little to Marx's own theories, which are still unsurpassed as an analysis of the workings of capitalism. Of course, some of them need updating—to accommodate globalization, for instance, and the digital world. But Marx has been widely read, not least by his opponents, and many of his insights have come to convince us now. In my view, the Marxist theory of ideology still helps to explain why things don't seem to get better faster.

Moreover, they argue, in order to represent its own interests as the shared values of all members of the society in question, the ruling class has to invest its views with the character of universality. We might now reflect on the fact that universal suffrage is the product of the capitalist epoch. In our own period, in other words, the form of ownership is freely chosen by everyone, at least officially, though always from within ideology. Capitalism becomes inevitable, natural.

'Ideological State Apparatuses'

Under capitalism the state sets up institutions to defend ownership. The most obvious of these are the law, the police force, and the prison system. When in 1969 Louis Althusser reread (or rewrote) *The German Ideology* in the light of Saussure and semiology, as well as Marx's own later work, he began from law enforcement. The Repressive State Apparatus preserves the existing relations of production that mean some people have to sell their labour-power to earn a living, and some don't but can rely on their property or investments. When it is directly challenged by crime, revolution, or civil disobedience, the Repressive State Apparatus works by force.

But many, or perhaps most, of us barely come into contact or collision with the police and the courts. We 'work by ourselves', Althusser says, to reproduce the class relations capitalism depends on, even if these do not serve our long-term interests. The deserving poor of the 19th century reaffirmed the values of that society, even though by doing so they mostly remained poor. Why?

Because, in Althusser's account, the Repressive State Apparatus finds a parallel in the Ideological State Apparatuses (ISAs), institutions that produce and reproduce the meanings and values which represent the relationship we imagine we have to our real conditions of existence. The ISAs tell us that we are free to get another job if we don't like this one; that work well done is a pleasure; that we can move to Venezuela if we don't like capitalism.

Louis Althusser, 1918–90

Professor of Philosophy at the École Normale Supérieure in Paris. Althusser reread the works of Marx in the light of 20th-century theoretical developments, including linguistics and psychoanalysis.

In *For Marx* (1965) he put forward the theory that society could best be understood as working on three levels: economic, political, and ideological. Each of these levels had a degree of independence, or 'relative autonomy', but each was also the condition of existence of the others, though they would not all necessarily move at the same rate. The motor of change was contradiction in or between the three levels. In line with Marx's own view that the form of ownership defined social relations, Althusser maintained that the economy was determining 'in the last instance'. But, conversely, the economy could never be finally isolated from the other two levels, so 'the lonely hour of the "last instance" never comes'. The ideology that did most to sustain capitalism was humanism, the belief in 'man' as the free, autonomous origin of history.

His essay 'Ideology and Ideological State Apparatuses' was published in 1969. This developed the attention given to ideology in *For Marx*, seeing it as the means of reproducing the relations of production (class struggle).

Prone to depression, in 1980 Althusser murdered his wife and was subsequently confined to a psychiatric institution. His autobiography, *The Future Lasts a Long Time* (1992), tells his version of the story.

None of this is simply false: ideology is not a set of delusions foisted on the stupid. But most of it isn't exactly the whole truth either. A zero-hours contract might not be freely chosen if it's the only work on offer. For a night office cleaner, especially if she has small children, work probably isn't much of a pleasure most of the time and, without qualifications, the available alternatives might not be any better. Her life in Venezuela would almost certainly be worse.

Althusser's list of ISAs includes religion, the family, the political system of elections and parties to choose from, the unions (insofar as they set out to improve the existing order, but not to change it), the media, sport, literature and the arts, and, supremely, education. These institutions, while not homogeneous in their output, and not without internal conflict, sometimes bitter, have the effect of securing our conscious or unconscious consent to the way things are, by making them appear at best in our interests and at worst inevitable. Above all, they seem *obvious*.

Discussions of capitalism often reach an impasse. Could there be a kinder form of ownership? When I raise this question, my interlocutors commonly assume that I must want to go back to Soviet communism. What else could there be? This is an instance of ideology at work: capitalism is better than communism, *obviously*, and an alternative to both is apparently unimaginable.

Those of us who were involved in teaching in the 1970s, when Althusser's essay on the ISAs first appeared in translation, were thrilled to learn that the education system was the main ideological apparatus. This meant that, as radicals, we had work to do on our own doorstep. The argument was that schools and universities not only eject a proportion of the young prepared to take up occupations at every level of the economic structure, but in the process of teaching reading, writing, and arithmetic, they also provide instruction in obedience, deference, elementary psychology, the virtues of liberal democracy, how to give or take orders, and how to serve the community. In short, they inculcate the discipline—and the self-discipline—that encourages their products to 'work by themselves'.

Ideology secures the system by consent. It is not a conspiracy; its reaffirmation is not deliberate. George Eliot's Adam Bede doesn't set out to confirm inequality. On the contrary, he simply does his duty and takes pleasure in his work. But it is exactly the sense of duty and pleasure that mask the element of exploitation involved in the fact that he has to sell his labour-power (he can't afford not to) for a wage which is less than his employer will get for the coat of arms he is carving, and much less than its purchasers probably earn from the rents they impose.

Adam Bede doesn't set out to mask exploitation either. But by showing the scene in its ideal form, and presenting inequality as inevitable, obvious, this 'realist' novel does in practice reproduce the imaginary relations of individuals to their real conditions of existence.

The subject

Does this mean that George Eliot should be roundly condemned for colluding with exploitation? Of course not. The moral praise-and-blame school of literary criticism (just *how* anti-feminist was D. H. Lawrence? how racist or anti-Semitic was Shakespeare?) has not taken account of the Death of the Author. George Eliot is not the origin or the explanation of the cultural convictions her novel reproduces. Besides, *Adam Bede* is remarkably sympathetic towards its working-class hero. The text is an effect of the meanings and values in circulation at its own historical moment.

Adam Bede (who does not exist), George Eliot (who is not his origin), and the unsuspecting reader (the one who has not carried out a semiological analysis) participate in a shared practice that contributes to the reproduction of the ruling ideology. These three figures are all, Althusser would say, subjects.

The subject is in the first place the subject of a sentence, the agent of the verb, and the figure that says 'I'. I reproduce (or challenge) the ruling ideology when I speak or write, and I am in that sense a source of initiatives, actions, decisions, choices. But at the same

The subject

Q. Isn't this a bit depressing? It makes us all out to be no better than conditioned robots.

A. It does imply that we're not necessarily the sole origin of our deepest convictions. But we can make choices and our views can change. How? It's the *ruling* ideology that confirms the way things are. Althusser's essay is mainly about the workings of ideology in general, but specific ideologies can challenge the ruling values (Marxism for one, poststructuralism for another). We don't have to insist on what's obvious. Indeed, the obvious is often incoherent when you try to think it through. Contradictions in the ruling ideology produce dissent, new beliefs, alternative subject-positions. (There will be more to say about dissent in Chapter 6.)

Running through the ISAs essay is a series of references to class struggle. As a Marxist, Althusser took for granted that all societies that are divided by class (which is to say, all societies hitherto) are propelled forwards by conflict, including theoretical disagreement. He wanted to privilege Marxism itself as a source of truth, so he called it 'science'. But a certain anxiety about this term pervades his work in its entirety. He was too good a philosopher to suppose that you could combine certainty with Saussure. Ideology itself is always a site of struggle.

So, incidentally, is the subject. How coherent are your beliefs and values? Have you never found you affirmed two convictions which can't both be true? I have—and sometimes in the same conversation.

time the subject is *subjected* to the meanings and sentence structures that language permits. I communicate *subject to* my reproduction of the accepted signifiers. We might want to argue (although Althusser doesn't explicitly) that the subject is shaped by citationality. The ambiguity of the subject's status, as agent and as subjected being, defines the use of the term.

The subject, Althusser maintains, is the destination of all ideology, and the place where ideology is reproduced. This is the source of its power: ideology is internal; we are its effects; we cite it unwittingly every time we reaffirm the 'obvious'.

Ideology or myth?

Clearly, there is considerable overlap between what Barthes calls 'myth' and what Althusser means by 'ideology'. Which term should we adopt?

'Ideology' indicates a Marxist allegiance. But because the same signifier is in common use to define a consciously held doctrine ('conservative ideology'), rather than what is, on the one hand, so obvious that it goes without saying and, on the other, the location of incoherences, contradictions, and political struggle, it is often necessary to explain how you are using the word before getting on with the argument.

Moreover, not all Marxists agree about its definition. Before Althusser published his essay, 'ideology' was commonly equated with 'false consciousness'. In Althusser the boundary between true and false is not so clearly marked. Ideology may present an 'imaginary' picture of the relations of production, but because it is lived in our everyday experience, it is not simply a delusion which can be shaken off once we recognize the truth. And how, in the light of Saussure's account of language, could we be sure it *was* the truth, anyway?

'Myth', too, is equivocal. Greek myths are fictions, we would now say. But we might also recognize that they were attempts to make sense of the world. Myths are not just for entertainment, but stories of how things came to be the way they are. For the culture that subscribes to them, they have explanatory power.

Roland Barthes's use of the term was a tribute to one of the major intellectual figures of the time, certainly the greatest mythographer of his generation, the anthropologist Claude Lévi-Strauss. Rejecting the ethnocentrism characteristic of an earlier generation of anthropologists, Lévi-Strauss refused to think of tribal cultures as 'primitive'. On the contrary, what interested him was the meaning of their customs, and the common ground between their everyday practices and ours.

Take the widespread tribal custom of *potlatch*, for example, where gifts are exchanged between families or communities. Each gift is expected to be more lavish than the previous one, and the competition creates mounting disequilibrium. This practice, Lévi-Strauss suggests, has parallels in the modern Western Christmas, where the quantity and the value of the cards ritually exhibited on the mantelpiece during the festival testify to the recipient's worth. Presents are expected to reach a certain standard (children become adept at exploiting the competitive element here), and at the end of the holiday a number of family budgets face radical disequilibrium.

This example comes from Lévi-Strauss's first book, *The Elementary Structures of Kinship*, published in French in 1949. Here he argues that all cultures have rules about marriageability, so that their members are divided into two categories, prohibited partners and possible partners. Marriage within these rules constitutes a fundamental form of exchange, and the project of exchange itself is 'reciprocity' as a way of overcoming hostility. Reciprocity means communication, alliance, integration, society itself. *Tristes Tropiques* in 1955 includes analyses of aspects of Amazonian art and ritual to show how they are intelligible to the ethnographer in terms of the local marriage rules.

To the ethnographer, but not to the practitioners themselves. Like *Mythologies*, which appeared in 1957, Lévi-Strauss's structural anthropology focuses on motivations that escape the gaze of the individuals concerned. It is not, he affirms, impossible for practitioners to become conscious of the implications of their own practices, the rituals and myths that cultures re-enact and reproduce, but such awareness represents the exception rather than the rule. Similarly, people who climb mountains may not set out to endorse the work ethic. Perhaps they just like the view from the top. But the view, Roland Barthes would say, is not the whole story.

Claude Lévi-Strauss, 1908–2009

Professor of Social Anthropology at the Collège de France 1959–82. Lévi-Strauss, who claimed to have chosen ethnography in order to avoid philosophy, became a professor at the University of São Paulo in Brazil in 1935. From there he did the field work among the native peoples of South America that led to his books. These include *The Savage Mind* (1962) and *The Raw and the Cooked* (1964). *Tristes Tropiques* is unique, part autobiography, part travel writing and part non-technical anthropology, by turns witty and haunting, always eloquent and thoroughly readable.

His efforts to evade philosophy were not entirely successful. Treating institutional and cultural differences as reducible to binary oppositions given in the mind, his writing ultimately proposed an account of human nature itself.

Anthropology offers a solution to the problem of terminology. In the end, its topic is neither mythology nor ideology, but culture. That signifier is not without its problems too, of course, but it has the effect of implicating us all in the common practices of our society, which are neither true nor false, but carry meanings and values we may not have chosen deliberately.

Structuralism or poststructuralism?

Were Barthes and Althusser simply applying the findings of structural anthropology to their own culture, then?

They certainly borrowed its account of determinations that escape our conscious awareness, but there is at least one crucial difference. In looking below the surface appearance of things, Lévi-Strauss wanted to find the common element of all cultures, traceable ultimately to universal structures embedded deep in the human mind. In his structuralist account, all myths are in the end transformations of each other, and all marriage customs reducible to the great duality of the incest taboo, where everyone is ruled either in or out as a potential partner. The founding principle of human culture in general is exchange, transforming hostility into reciprocity.

His quest, in other words, was for Eternal Man, that fantasy figure of bourgeois ideology, the single, continuous hero of history masquerading as nature. Structuralism was extremely seductive. Speculative and far-reaching, it promised a key to all human practices, a mastery of the single principle that would hold together the apparently disparate features of all cultures. But it treated difference as no more than superficial, and difference was the key term in Saussure's revolutionary theory of language.

At roughly this time, Noam Chomsky began work on his theory of universal grammar. During the heady days of the 1950s and 1960s, structuralism was everywhere. It moved easily from myth to stories. Barthes himself produced an essay on 'The Structural

Analysis of Narratives'. As early as 1928, the Russian Formalist Vladimir Propp had analysed the fairy tales of his own culture, ignoring the variables to find a single structure of seven possible characters and 31 possible actions. *The Morphology of the Folktale* first appeared in English in 1958, eliciting an essay from Lévi-Strauss himself in 1960. He praised Propp as a forerunner, but pointed out that the problem with formalism was its policy of ignoring thematic content. When in 1966 A.-J. Greimas published the ambitious *Structural Semantics*, he brought together Saussure and Lévi-Strauss to rewrite Propp for structuralism. What he found was a pattern for all stories, centring on the conflict between the hero's quest for individual freedom and the constraints of the existing order.

At just that time, Jacques Derrida wrote critically about the nostalgia Lévi-Strauss displays for a lost human wholeness, as well as the binary oppositions his case both depends on and fails to sustain. But perhaps the most explicit textual moment of poststructuralism came in 1970 at the beginning of *S/Z*, Roland Barthes's anarchic, infinitely suggestive and still unsurpassed close reading of a Balzac story. Apropos, apparently, of nothing in particular, *S/Z* begins, 'There are said to be certain Buddhists whose ascetic practices enable them to see a whole landscape in a bean.' This rumination then continues:

> Precisely what the first analysts of narrative were attempting: to see all the world's stories (and there have been ever so many) within a single structure: we shall, they thought, extract from each tale its model, then out of these models we shall make a great narrative structure, which we shall reapply (for verification) to any one narrative: a task as exhausting...as it is ultimately undesirable, for the text thereby loses its difference.

Suddenly, the grand claims of structuralism appear absurd. Once you have found the single determining structure, there is nothing to choose between the universe and a bean. The microcosm takes its place as an illustration of the general scheme, another instance of the same pattern, thrilling for the system-builders, but then what? What can further investigation discover? Only endless repetition. The big questions have been answered in advance.

How ironic, then, Barthes goes on, that Saussure's attribution of meaning to difference should lead in the end to the equalization of all texts 'under the scrutiny of an in-different science' (in-different because undifferentiating, but also indifferent because in the end apathetic, bored).

When *S/Z* itself sets up five 'codes' as the universal framework of its textual analysis, the process suggests a parody of structuralism, not least because the brilliant 'divagations' (wanderings) of *S/Z*'s own analysis keep on leaving them behind. At the same time, these purely formal codes set out to specify a set of relationships between the text and the reader, and within them Balzac's story is shown to have some quite remarkable themes, which are certainly neither universal nor eternal.

Is *Mythologies* poststructuralist?

If *Mythologies* belongs in a line of descent from structural anthropology, is it right to class it as poststructuralist? Insofar as the question matters at all (and perhaps in the end it doesn't, much), my answer would be yes and no.

Lévi-Strauss looked, he said, for the invariant element among superficial differences. To a degree, Barthes does that too: the confusion of history with nature is the recurring theme. But this concern is not itself universal or invariant. On the contrary, it belongs specifically to our own bourgeois moment, and has nothing whatever to do with structures deep in the human mind.

Besides, *Mythologies* frequently seems to forget that this is its topic. Though the essays are all to varying degrees sceptical about the myths they analyse, and interested in drawing surprising parallels, they are not concerned to reduce them to a single theme. Lévi-Strauss's method is invoked—but in order to draw attention to historical and individual differences.

And Althusser?

What about the ISAs essay? Is that structuralist, or poststructuralist? This much more abstract thesis concerns ideology in general, with examples drawn from bourgeois ideology. Here again a case could be made either way. But what points forward in Althusser's work is the element of struggle involved in constantly renewing (reproducing) the obviousnesses that sustain the existing relations of production. Education may be the most powerful of the ISAs, but even here there are teachers who (heroically) resist promoting what is reactionary in the curriculum.

It is implicit in Althusser's analysis that ideology is divided against itself. And if ideology is in this sense *other than it is*, so is the subject that is its effect and support. The subject, then, is our next concern.

Chapter 3
The differed subject

In February 1868, in a miserable lodging house, Abel Barbin died of carbon dioxide asphyxiation from a charcoal stove. Abel, who was 29 years old, and worked in a railway office in Paris, left a memoir which testifies both to his high intelligence and to the desolation that led to his suicide. It appears that he was caught between two jobs, neither of which matched his abilities or took account of his experience. Friendless in the French capital, and frequently unemployed, convinced, meanwhile, that he had no chance of the companionship and sexual satisfaction marriage would offer, he saw his existence as useless to others and crushing to himself.

Abel, who was baptized Adelaide-Herculine Barbin, had grown up as a girl. She had spent most of her life in all-female institutions and, after coming top in the examinations, had gone on to teach in a girls' boarding school. There she fell in love with another teacher, gradually recognizing, to her own surprise, the nature of this passion, which was consummated in due course. The two shared a bed for many months, until the suspicions of those around them, as well as the falseness of their position, prompted Adelaide-Herculine to consult a priest. When he passed her on to the medical authorities, the doctor found a person of slight but broadly masculine appearance, with rudimentary versions of the genital organs of both sexes. There was no womb.

In 1860, at the age of 21, Adelaide-Herculine was re-registered officially as Abel, and lived from then on as a man. This was binary thinking: if not one sex, then the other. The early parts of the memoir, somewhat literary and sentimental, nevertheless clearly depict a girlhood of relative social integration and considerable academic success. When it goes on to tell Abel's story, however, the text becomes rambling and repetitive.

Even so, it is clear that Abel feels alone and disgraced, unable to return to those who have known him as a woman. More aware, now, of what is expected sexually, he sees no hope of a future relationship to match the first. Meanwhile, the jobs he applies for demand experience. Abel's experience has been as a schoolmistress, but at this period a teaching post in a girls' school was not an option for a man. To his shame, Abel is reduced to asking his poverty-stricken mother for money.

Socialized, culturally shaped in a 19th-century world where sexual roles were dramatically polarized, Herculine/Abel cannot survive as either a woman or a man. Once recruited as a woman by the meanings of femininity she has done her best to inhabit, she has the utmost difficulty in becoming a different, masculine subject, sharing and reproducing the meanings that make possible conventional male behaviour. The contrast between the forms of subjectivity appropriate to men and women could hardly have been more extreme than it was at this time. It is easy to see, though the author of the memoir cannot theorize it, how difficult it would be, both socially and psychologically, to become a member of the opposite sex in such circumstances.

Virginia Woolf made high comedy out of the reverse transformation in her fantasy novel *Orlando* in 1928. Waking up to find herself suddenly, as if by magic, a woman, after growing up as a man, Orlando has to learn to cope with the difficulty of getting around in skirts, retreating where she has been accustomed to pursue, choosing whether to yield or refuse, when she has habitually insisted. Now she finds that women are not 'obedient, chaste, scented and exquisitely apparelled by nature'. Instead, they can only acquire these virtues 'by the most tedious discipline', and Orlando reluctantly sets about the task.

Herculine Barbin's predicament was no joke, however. It was not eased by the insistence of her priest and the medical profession that she must be reassigned to her 'true' sex. Abel could not simply banish Herculine, who survived the abrupt transition as an inner difference.

Though many people are now mercifully more relaxed about gender, some have remained ill at ease with intersex babies, and doctors have sometimes taken it upon themselves to determine the 'true' sex of such children, risking their resistance in later life. Traditional Western culture has decreed that there are two sexes. While in a number of other languages pronouns are not gendered, English, as the inscription of a culture, conventionally offers two possibilities, masculine and feminine. People who reject the binary distinction increasingly opt to be called 'they', not only stripping sexual difference of its cultural weight but allowing a hint of plurality to disrupt our rigid classifications.

Brought into line

Cultural norms change—and not always for the better. On the one hand, Western culture now celebrates same-sex relationships and acknowledges the limitations of binary gender-identifications. On the other, marketing makes the old opposition more pressing than ever. In the 1980s we were less inclined to dress our babies in *either* pink or blue. Plenty of yellows and greens were available to avoid the issue. However, as the waters close over, department stores once again offer pretty pink dresses or jaunty blue romper suits. If women wear unisex trousers without comment, men in skirts can still raise eyebrows. Many trans people adhere to one side or the other of a sharp binary line.

Free subjects?

Gender-identification is only one instance of the way people in liberal societies perceive themselves as free, permitted to proclaim their views, however eccentric—or ex-centric—and entitled to challenge the existing order if they wish. Anyone, we claim proudly, can refuse to conform. But ex-centricity soon encounters limits. Outright refusal of the conventions may still get people classified as oddballs and risk disqualifying the challenges they deliver. The man in a suit commands assent more readily than the unkempt homeless woman shouting at the traffic.

In the memoir, although it was Abel who did the writing, the narrative voice that recounts the convent girlhood is not characteristic of a man. Lives are narratable as coherent in terms of the categories language makes available. The story of Herculine, as told by Herculine herself, makes sense. But at the point in the story when she ceases to be what language and culture have made of her, the writing collapses into incoherence. Neither a woman nor a man, since Abel has no male experience, habits, bonds, ways of thinking of himself, in short, no *history*, this newly created figure can say 'I', but without being able to attach to the pronoun an intelligible sentence beyond something like '... am poor, lonely, and very unhappy'.

Identity can be conceived as a set of characteristics, or a social role, as recognition of belonging to a circle, or as membership of a group. In all these senses, Abel has lost one identity without managing to find another. Herculine/Abel's specific tragedy was socially produced, the result of a requirement, that we would surely find unjust, to adhere to a single, recognized identity.

Would the solution have been an alternative—intersex—identity? Identity presupposes a unified, stable individual. Herculine/Abel could find no such unity or stability but occupied, poststructuralism would say, conflicting subject-positions—as woman, man, or neither, capable, defenceless, or both. A new identity would risk collapsing such differences. Socially imposed as it is, identity simplifies. In our own time Herculine Barbin might hope to find a more sympathetic priest and a more imaginative doctor, as well as a circle of allies. To be most convincing, the case made by this group would be based on justice, not the restrictive category of identity.

The subject of a sentence is the person (or thing) who enacts the verb: 'Herculine was a schoolteacher'; 'Abel looked for work.' A subject takes a position by uttering, even if only by implication, a sentence using 'I': 'I want a job,' or 'I am no longer the only person I have learnt how to be.'

As a free subject, I plan my life (within certain obvious constraints), affirm my values, choose my friends (if they'll have me) and give an account of myself: 'I am...this or that.' But I make myself intelligible on the understanding that to a certain degree I invoke (*subject* myself to) the terms, categories, and conventions that I and others recognize. Subjects in isolation have

'Subject' and 'identity'

'Subject' is more precise than 'identity'. First, as a grammatical category, it places the emphasis squarely on the language we learn from birth, source of the meanings, including the meanings of 'man' and 'woman' our culture expects us to live by. Second, it builds in the ambiguity of the grammatical term itself: I am free to claim attention to the degree that I accept a certain subjection to those cultural norms. And third, it allows for discontinuities and contradictions. I can occupy a range of subject-positions, and not all of them will necessarily be consistent with each other. 'Identity' lays claim to sameness: that's what the word means. Subjects can differ—even from themselves.

only a limited power to remake the meanings they have internalized in the process of learning their native language. Together, however, they can bring about a shift of values.

Foucault

Michel Foucault, who assembled the archive in *Herculine Barbin*, devoted most of his history of knowledges and practices to analysing the effects of culture in requiring subjects to give an account of themselves. The categories we all recognize not only make this account possible but also *call us* to account, and by doing so bring us into line with the norms and proprieties that culture itself constructs. Cultures recruit us as subjects, subject us to their values, and incite us to be responsible citizens, eager, indeed, to identify ourselves in terms and behaviours we have learnt from the signifying practices of those cultures themselves.

Foucault's *Discipline and Punish*, first published in French in 1975, considers the ways societies have penalized those who rejected their norms. In absolutist France, for instance, criminals were publicly tortured and executed, and the book begins with a detailed and gruesome record of the punishment of a regicide in 1757. Foucault juxtaposes this with the regulations of an institution for young offenders in the mid-19th century. The rules prescribe the exact distribution of their time: up at six; five minutes to dress in silence; another five to make their beds; work until ten and then a meal, after washing their hands; school at twenty to eleven for two hours; and so on, until bed-time at eight-thirty.

Compared with the spectacle of public execution, where the state demonstrated on the body of the criminal its cruel power to punish those who challenged the sovereign, the penal institution looks more humane, more lenient, and more constructive. And so, of course, in an obvious sense, it is. But its agenda is a discipline that subjects the inmates, body and soul, to a regime designed precisely to construct them as conforming citizens, which is to say *subjects*, in both senses of that term, who learn to work by themselves in submission to the values of their society.

Resistance

Which of these two regimes allows more scope for resistance? Ironically, the first, Foucault argues. Punished in public, criminals who behaved courageously sometimes became popular heroes. Ballads were circulated giving their side of the story. Crowds occasionally turned on the executioner. But hidden away and trained to internalize new disciplines, prisoners were more effectively brought into line, to emerge as docile subjects, the fight drilled out of them.

All relations, Foucault argued, are in this sense relations of power, which does not belong only to the state. Parents and teachers subject children when they socialize them. Professions set exams and in the process define the knowledges required to join them. Employment depends on people keeping time and obeying instruction. This is not a matter of individual intention or wish. Learning entails submission; work demands routine.

Norms, then, are culturally produced and, to the degree that they constitute regimes, represent a form of subjection. In Foucault's account, power is creative: it produces ways of being and ideals to aspire to. In his later work, including the massive history of sexuality he planned but never completed, he began to name as 'bio-power' the management of bodies in the administration of life. Where the medieval sovereign possessed the power to kill enemies, the modern state works to measure and regulate the population in terms of birth rates, vigour, and longevity, with special attention to sexual health. Sex becomes an object of knowledge, the classification of sexual practices and identities a cause of surveillance and self-surveillance. Norms produce disciplined subjects.

But does this mean we cannot resist our own subjection? No, of course not, though there might be a price to pay. There is by definition no power without the possibility of resistance, Foucault insists, and the word carries heroic overtones for a generation that remembered with admiration the dangers incurred by the refusal of the French underground to submit to the Nazi occupation. Resistance is power's defining difference. Crime itself is a refusal of the law; 'vice' is a rejection of conventional ethics. Power is not a thing or a quantity we possess or lose, but a relation of struggle, sometimes within the individual. Foucault's own work is full of doomed heroes: murderers, madmen, and suicides who resisted their own subjection.

Sexual norms

Among Foucault's most influential propositions was the argument put forward in the first volume of *The History of Sexuality* that homosexuality did not exist until the 19th century.

But surely the Greeks practised homosexuality? Not exactly, Foucault would reply. Certainly, men had sexual relations with boys or men, just as they have done in many other cultures. But they were not in consequence classified as homosexuals, invested with a subjectivity that was seen as the origin of their sexual practices, let alone named as deviant or perverse. They did not consider themselves defined by their sexual activities.

The effect of the relatively recent process of classifying sexual subjects, Foucault indicates, was twofold. On the one hand, it tended to limit the range of available forms of pleasure. Once you feel an obligation to come out, if only to yourself, to *decide* whether you are gay or straight, you declare a preference that constrains your choices, however unconsciously. On the other hand, as soon as the category exists, you can defend it, insist on its rights, call for justice with others who feel oppressed by the norm, invoking what Foucault calls a 'reverse discourse' as the basis of resistance to the norm itself.

Psychoanalysis

Poststructuralism is not a system, nor even, when you look at the details, a unified body of theory. How could it be? Its key term is difference.

The Marxist Louis Althusser urged that, as the destination of ideology, subjects 'work by themselves' to reproduce it unless they choose to resist. Michel Foucault's account overlapped with Althusser's, but emphasized the role of knowledges and practices in recruiting subjects. On the other hand, Foucault rejected Marxism as another kind of 'discipline', a self-proclaimed 'truth' that aligned subjects with its own norms. Foucault was deeply suspicious of all such truths. On similar grounds, he also deplored psychoanalysis, because it co-opts us in the name of the truth of our innermost being, understood to be sexual. It was, after all, the reassignment of Herculine Barbin to her 'true' sex that destroyed her.

Foucault's is a familiar way of reading Freud, but not the only possible one. Post-war Paris was a place of many rereadings. If Roland Barthes reread Lévi-Strauss in the light of Saussure, Althusser even more explicitly reread Marx in the light of psychoanalysis to produce his account of ideology. But his version of psychoanalysis was already itself a Lacanian rereading of Freud. No wonder no one agreed with the exact details of anyone else's view!

Jacques Lacan did not promise the truth; nor did he see sex as the origin of the self; but he did reinterpret Freud in the light of Saussure (and Lévi-Strauss) to delineate a subject that was itself the location of difference. Lacan's subject is divided against itself, 'other', he says, 'than it is', dissatisfied—and desiring.

Prohibitions

Lacanian psychoanalysis takes from Freud the idea of the forbidding Father (with a capital F, because this figure is a structural position rather than the actual person who romps with the kids or helps them do their homework). Lacan is enough of a Freudian to retain the idea that children desire *everything* (including their mothers). The linchpin of the culture they must learn to obey is the Father, who says 'no' to most of what they want (especially their mothers). Lacan inscribes this point in a pun that works only in French. When we learn language, we submit to the *Non/Nom* that the Father bequeaths us, his 'no', as well as his name.

In a sense, 'good' subjects take on both, inheriting the Father's values along with the language that names him. That is to say, we assume a place in society on condition that we reproduce the signifying practices derived from culture as the big Other. Lacan calls this the symbolic order: 'symbolic' because signifiers are symbols, and 'order' because language is a discipline that recruits and forbids in one breath. But that discipline does not do away with desire.

The subject of desire

Why is it that the grand love stories, those that become legendary when so many get forgotten, tend to be the ones with unhappy endings? Many people in Western culture probably know the stories of more than one of the following: Dido and Aeneas, Antony and Cleopatra, Tristan and Isolde, Lancelot and Guinevere, Romeo and Juliet, Anna Karenina, *Brief Encounter*, *Casablanca*.

Why do we remember them? Or why have some of the older ones been recycled so many times in opera, novels, and films? Is it that unfulfilled desire for some reason strikes a particular chord? Lacan would say so.

For Lacan the human being is an organism-in-culture, and the disjunction that implies is the source of our troubles. We are born organisms (of course), and we become subjects. How? By adopting the *Non/Nom* of the Father, internalizing the order that surrounds us from the moment we come into the world. We turn into subjects in the process of learning language, which means that we become capable of signifying. This is an advantage: we can ask for what we want instead of crying helplessly, and go on to catch the right bus, post messages on social media, make political speeches—or read Lacan, of course, according to taste.

But the language that permits all this is irretrievably Other. Lacan uses a capital O to distinguish the Otherness of language and culture from the otherness of other people, though of course it is from people that we learn and internalize the Otherness of the signifier. They, too, however, are its subjects.

The big Other is there before we are, exists outside us, and does not belong to us. In the course of asking for what we want, for instance, we necessarily borrow our terms from the Other, since we have no alternative if we want to communicate. In this way, the little human organism, which begins with no sense of a distinction between itself and the world, gets separated off from its surroundings, and is obliged to formulate its demands in terms of the differences already available in language, however alienating these might be.

Something is lost here, creating a lack in the speaking being. Unconscious desire arises from the alienating process of speaking in terms that belong to the Other. But the unconscious itself also belongs to the Other as it sets out to signify on behalf of a desire that remains unknown to the subject. That desire returns to disturb and disrupt our subjection to what Lacan calls 'the goods': the codes and proprieties recognized as virtuous. The unconscious that makes its effects felt in dreams, slips of the tongue, puns, jokes, or symptoms marked on the body is also 'the discourse of the Other'. Unconscious desire impels resistance: we should never, Lacan insists, give up on it.

Desire, in Lacan's account, is for nothing nameable, since desire is unconscious and its object not knowable. But it is structural, the consequence of loss, and thus a perpetual condition, the effect of a lack in being. Although the first object of desire is irretrievably lost, most of us find a succession of substitutes, and fasten our desire onto them, as if they could make us whole again, heal the rift in the subject. In the end, they can't—though, of course, it's possible to have a good time in the process of finding that out.

Venus

Lacan would have approved of Titian's Venuses. I went to my first exhibition of Titian's paintings with no particular expectations, except that it would be pleasurable. In the event, I walked slowly round the gallery in a daze, came out at the end of the exhibition, and immediately joined the queue to go round again. I had never seen so much desire in a single space. Even the portraits seemed to stare wistfully out of the canvas, at an angle to the spectator, as if they could see something in the distance that they couldn't have and we couldn't name.

Venus Blindfolding Cupid shows the goddess of love punishing her son for shooting his arrows apparently at random (see Figure 4). Ironically, her action is only likely to make things worse: a blind Cupid will surely act even more anarchically. But Venus does not appear to be concentrating on her task. She looks off to the left, apparently at nothing in particular, her expression suggesting that her daydream does not give her much satisfaction. Meanwhile, the other winged putto looks sadly over her shoulder, perhaps pitying Cupid, or possibly foreseeing his own fate.

Maybe Venus herself is the victim of Cupid's arrow here. It wouldn't be the only time. In Shakespeare's *Venus and Adonis*, the goddess falls in love with a beautiful but indifferent mortal, who prefers hunting. The poem draws attention to the paradox of her role: 'She's love, she loves, and yet she is not loved.' As the goddess of love, Venus is not only the supreme object of desire but its subject too, capable of more than mortal longings. The poem ends by making the story into a fable of the origin of desire's pain. Disappointed, Venus curses love and, as the personification of the condition, she has the power to make her curse come true. From now on, she announces, passion will always be full of anguish.

4. The goddess of love is subject to desire.

Lacan thought so too. There is, he insisted, no such thing as perfect sexual rapport. In Lacanian theory it is not some fundamental sexual imperative that motivates desire, however, but incompleteness, lack. We can see, Lacan argues, how sexual relationships come to 'occupy' the field of desire, since they involve the signifier at its most lyrical, as well as the organism at its most sensitive, but they are not its source. Indeed, they are not its solution either, since the signifier and the organism often pull in different directions.

Perhaps in the end the most compelling passion, the one that is never gratified, is not sexual at all but the desire to know for sure, the longing to push back the limits imposed by the Otherness of the symbolic order and gain, as subjects, unmediated access to the world.

Jacques Lacan, 1901–81

Psychoanalyst who radically reinterpreted Freud in the light of linguistics and anthropology. His *Écrits* (1966) are extraordinarily elusive, cryptic, and dense at first reading. Lacan's annual Seminars, conducted in Paris from 1953–4 onwards, have been gradually appearing, first in French and then in translation. These are less obscure, but only marginally so.

The writings and these oral deliveries were addressed to psychoanalysts, whose job it was, Lacan believed, to listen extremely attentively to what their patients said. The role of the analyst is to hear the voice of the unconscious, which makes itself audible through the censorship of consciousness in riddles, allusions, elisions, and omissions. Lacan's own riddling manner mimics the utterances of the unconscious.

For his admirers, the style makes his texts themselves into objects of desire. 'This time,' I always think, 'I'm going to get it straight.' If only. But it becomes easier. And it is worth it. Lacan was enormously well-read and highly intelligent. His incidental comments on painting, architecture, tragedy, for instance, are often worth whole volumes of more ponderous scholarship.

Strangers to ourselves?

Facing exile, Thomas Mowbray in Shakespeare's *Richard II* complains that in a foreign country his tongue will become like a musical instrument that has lost its strings. Julia Kristeva's *Strangers to Ourselves* is about foreignness. It begins with a moving, poetic account of what it's like to be an immigrant, cherishing 'that language of the past that withers without ever leaving you'. You improve your skills in the new one, but it's never quite *yours*, and you lack the authority that goes with unthinking fluency. You are easy to ignore, and thus readily humiliated. Increasingly foreign to those you have left behind as well, you become a kind of cultural orphan, never *at one* with anyone anywhere.

At the same time, immigrants may suddenly find the prohibitions they have grown up with suspended as the power of the inherited symbolic order is lifted. They become 'liberated', other than they are. But are they freer? Or just more solitary?

Why is it common to fear foreigners, people from other cultures, asylum seekers? Well, for one thing, they demonstrate that there are alternative ways to be, that our own ways are not inevitable, and therefore not necessarily 'natural'. Disparaging the others seems to make some people feel better. Besides, the encounter with foreigners calls in question the reassuring 'we' that is so easily taken for granted.

This 'we', like the individuals who comprise it, was always divided, Kristeva concludes. Psychoanalysis indicates that we are all foreign to ourselves. In the first place, there is something everyone has left behind:

> A child confides in his analyst that the finest day in his life is that of his birth: 'Because that day it was me—I like being me, I don't like being an other.' Now he feels other when he has poor grades—when

he is bad, alien to the parents' and teachers' desire. Likewise, the unnatural, 'foreign' languages, such as writing or mathematics, arouse an uncanny feeling in the child.

And in the second place, we are all inhabited by a stranger, whose ways are unknown to us, and contest the values we (think we) take for granted:

> The foreigner is within us. And when we flee from or struggle against the foreigner, we are fighting our unconscious—that 'improper' facet of our impossible 'own and proper'.

In these circumstances, one object of desire, especially familiar in a postcolonial world, is identity itself. Many people, especially those subject to a history of oppression, experience a longing to belong to a group that maintains its own unity against outsiders. And who, in a globalized world, is not at the mercy of institutions, corporations, a language defined or controlled elsewhere, experienced as other? Since at least the 19th century, nationalism has offered one way to restore a true identity that has been all but erased.

Jacques Derrida considers this claim in *Monolingualism of the Other*, first published in French in 1996. His own special case is French Algeria, where he grew up as a Jewish child in the 1930s. Ironically, Arabic was taught in the schools there as if it were a foreign language. Hebrew, meanwhile, was not taught at all. French was the young Derrida's first language, although this too was the property of others: it belonged in the faraway country of France.

And yet, in a sense, Derrida argues, his own case was exemplary for all of us. Culture is always 'colonial', in that it imposes itself by its power to name the world and to instil rules of conduct. No one inhabits a culture *by nature*. As a matter of definition, no culture comes naturally. We are all exiles. Moreover, the culture we belong to is never beyond improvement, never quite what it *should* be. Doesn't nationalism repudiate the nation as it has become, to identify with a fantasy vision of the land as it once was?

The masculine and feminine norms that excluded Abel Barbin were instilled by culture, not nature. Skin colour does not of itself entail particular allegiances. Identity is conferred by the big Other, not given in advance. The eventual effect of identity politics is to divide from one another groups who would otherwise recognize a common interest in resisting their own disadvantaged state. Identity politics can neither deliver the purity it promises nor form the basis of a fairer world. The support of the group can reinforce self-confidence and consolidate resistance but, in the end, the shared project must be justice.

It bears repeating: we are all exiles. At the same time, in the current world order we do well to remember that not all exiles are politically equivalent. Regrettably, some people, minorities and migrants among them, are more exiled than others…The big Other does not distribute power equally among the groups it distinguishes. In these cases, justice is still harder to come by— and all the more pressing for that.

Scandal

With Kristeva's proposition that we none of us know quite who we are, with Derrida's affirmation of our inevitable exile, Lacan's view that our dissatisfaction is structural, and Foucault's emphasis on resistance, poststructuralism has tended to have a certain radical edge. But no aspect of it has been more scandalous than its account of the subject. Constructed to a high degree by the big Other, subjected by meanings outside its control and even its consciousness, divided against itself as the effect of a loss, the subject of poststructuralism is neither unified nor an origin, and is thus a far cry from the unique individual who has traditionally represented humanity in the Free West.

By contrast, Western institutions, democratic electoral systems, and the market economy all assume that human beings are the independent source of meanings and choices. The freedom prized so highly is freedom to be whatever consciousness makes of us. In other words, Western 'common sense', itself a cultural construct, conspires to convince us that we are what we (freely) think.

The belief goes back nearly four centuries to René Descartes, the philosopher who affirmed, 'I think, therefore I am.' In a quest for the ultimate truth, Descartes set out to strip away any beliefs he could not be certain of. He was left with one conviction that, he claimed, could not be doubted: as the person doing the doubting, he at least must exist. On that basis, he was able to rebuild a philosophical system that, he insisted, owed nothing to outside authorities.

The Cartesian *cogito* (the 'I think') played a major part in promoting the scientific and rational development of the Enlightenment in the 18th century. These days, most philosophers would have some reservations about Descartes, but his famous phrase has become part of current Western common sense. Its effect is to conflate the self with what thinks. 'I' become primarily a consciousness, and that consciousness, in turn, is seen as the origin of 'my' ideas and values.

Poststructuralism, I have already suggested, questions the view that consciousness is an origin, treating it rather as an effect of signification: I owe to the big Other the meanings and differences that permit me to think at all. Psychoanalysis deepens the scandal by redoubling consciousness with unconscious desires that exercise other determinations, according to an agenda we don't even recognize. The free individual is no longer either individual or free.

Mind and body

Descartes claimed that, whereas he *was* a mind, he *had* a body. The two were radically distinct from one another. The organism had its own mechanical processes and reflexes, but reason was wholly independent of physiology. If we now take for granted that psychological tension causes headaches, or stress affects our immune system, we owe that recognition in part to psychoanalysis, which as early as the 1890s began attributing physical symptoms to unconscious desires.

But psychoanalysis does not on that account settle for the idea that a human being is best understood as an undifferentiated 'whole'. On the contrary: the relation between the organism and the subject is an uneasy one, to the degree that we become subjects at the price of an organic loss. This loss is not simply a single event in the past, but repeats itself throughout human life, and we subsist as an uneasy conjunction of organic impulses and cultural values, each at the expense of the other.

The term 'subject', then, is not just a jargon word for 'self'. While what we mean by 'the self' (or 'person' or 'individual') is generally the whole package, the subject is divided both within itself and from the organism. As what signifies, the subject is, on the one hand, conscious (rational, deliberate), and on the other hand, unconscious (motivated by desires that make themselves known only indirectly in dreams, slips, jokes, or symptoms). Meanwhile, this divided subject is inseparable from the body—when the organism dies the subject ceases to exist—but at the same time, it is distinguishable from the body, if only to the extent that each is conceivable only at the price of the loss of the other. As pure organism, I would not be a subject. At the same time, I cannot ever be pure subject, because I remain an organism.

We are born human beings, in that we are the offspring of two human parents; we become subjects as a result of cultural construction. But we are haunted by what culture does not know about us.

It's a hard life

With all these divisions in place, it's not always much fun being a subject. No wonder, then, that Abel Barbin decided he had had enough.

Herculine's body was more masculine than feminine but, as a subject, her cultural construction was more feminine than masculine. Falling in love, bringing the subject and the organism into joint action, created a crisis. Assigned to what the doctor called his true sex on the basis of his body, Abel was required to create a new subjectivity overnight. It couldn't be done, and he became confused, incoherent, depressed. If psychoanalysis is right about the unconscious, we none of us know quite what we mean when we say 'I'. Abel had this problem to the power of ten. Life in such circumstances seemed unliveable, and he put an end to it.

Oppositions

As the last paragraph makes particularly clear (I hope!), using the oppositions the symbolic order provides makes some things impossible to say with any accuracy. We cannot do justice to Herculine/Abel's story in terms of the names or pronouns on offer. How should we name this figure who, to compound the confusion, calls herself Alexina in her memoir? In this instance, 'they' stands to obscure the protagonist's abrupt and involuntary transformation. I have uncomfortably used the feminine forms for the early life and the masculine forms for the period after the reassignment.

The intersex person, Jacques Derrida might say, deconstructs the opposition between masculine and feminine, just as psychoanalysis, I would want to add, deconstructs the opposition between mind and body. But deconstruction is another story, and deserves a new chapter, beginning with the problem of truth.

Chapter 4
Difference or truth?

Jeanette Winterson's novel *Written on the Body* has an unnamed narrator whose gender is never revealed. Since this is a love story, the question is, you might think, material. The other central figure is a woman. Is this relationship heterosexual or lesbian? The novel doesn't say, though it drops hints that point sometimes this way, sometimes that.

Some readers, resisting the Death of the Author, assume that, since the book is written by a gay woman, the narrator must be a woman. They ignore the fact that 300 years ago Daniel Defoe impersonated a woman in *Moll Flanders*, or that substantial parts of Dickens's *Bleak House* are recounted by Esther Summerson. Emily Brontë, meanwhile, included narrators of both sexes in *Wuthering Heights*, beginning by impersonating Mr Lockwood. The difference is that in the modern (or postmodern?) novel, we can't be sure.

Sometimes it's genre that's in question. Toni Morrison's *Beloved* centres on a woman whose dead baby returns to disrupt her world. Are we to take this child's existence literally, or is she a projection, a way of acknowledging the implications for the African-American present of the unresolved past of slavery? Is the novel a ghost story or a latter-day allegory? Or is it, conversely, a more thought-provoking work if we don't decide?

When they introduce doubts without resolving them, by withholding a final truth, these novels come into line with the implications of Saussure's insights into language as I outlined them in Chapter 1. If signification is differential rather than referential, if we owe our ideas of things to differences that are in the first instance the effect of the symbolic order, we can never be certain of the truth. Some issues remain undecidable.

In other words, if the source of our perception of differences is signifying practice, not things in the world, there are no guarantees that our account of it arranges the world of things accurately. The most familiar notion of truth is that what we say corresponds to the actual state of affairs. But how, independent of the signifier, can we ascertain the state of affairs itself? If different languages divide the world up differently, and if different cultures lay claim to distinct beliefs, what, apart from habit, makes ours more true than theirs? Moreover, an increasingly multicultural West has come to acknowledge, however grudgingly, that it is possible to arrange things differently. Racism feeds on the widespread anxiety that, if other cultures manage with other world pictures, our own may not be as authoritative as we like to think.

This is not to say, of course, that Jeanette Winterson and Toni Morrison had diligently read Saussure or the poststructuralists, though it's possible. A more likely explanation is that, as so commonly in the history of culture, a number of causes converged to 'overdetermine' (the word comes from psychoanalysis, but was given new currency by Althusser) uncertainty about what we (think we) know. Throughout the 20th century new theoretical developments, including sociology, ethnology, and psychoanalysis itself, combined to indicate that beliefs might be the effect of motivations and allegiances we do not necessarily recognize.

The issue here is not what exists, but what we can accurately say exists. Faithful to Saussure, poststructuralism is concerned with what goes on at the level of the signifier. Truths (or otherwise) are told in language. Poststructuralist anxiety concerns not whether there is a world but what we can claim to say about it with certainty.

Many people today are willing to surrender the idea that there is in all instances a single, authoritative truth to be discovered and defended. Indeed, a century or more of political groups not only defending the truth as they perceived it but also initiating devastating violence against people who didn't share their convictions has left many of us ready to have serious doubts about the assertion of truth claims. Besides, travelling the global village, even if only on television or online, we encounter a wide range of world pictures. The young, in particular, are often willing to give up on truth.

The subject to the rescue?

But a common alternative is to hold that 'it's all subjective', or that truth exists as the property of the individual. 'It's what I believe', people say; 'it's true for *me*'. By this means they lay claim to a proper tolerance of other opinions, but at the same time they manage to hold on to the view that the individual consciousness is the place where ambiguities are resolved. If unmediated and unmotivated access to objective facts is not an option, truth, they assume, must be a purely personal matter.

The poststructuralist alternative

Poststructuralism looks at the question differently. In the first place, if the subject is an effect of culture, a result of the circulation of meanings in the symbolic order, and not their origin, subjectivity is more likely to reproduce the uncertainties and the range of beliefs we encounter than to resolve them. How many people do you know whose opinions are all entirely clear-cut and, at the same time, compatible with each other? Are your own views wholly consistent? My friend Susan's aren't, despite her best efforts. She has no religious convictions, because she doesn't see any reason to believe in the supernatural. At the same time, she's very reluctant to walk under ladders, and always reads her horoscope.

And in the second place, the distinction between the subject in here and the object out there is itself the consequence of the old view of the relationship between human beings and language. If, in the Cartesian tradition of the Enlightenment, my consciousness is what exists unconditionally, and language is no more than the instrument it makes use of to communicate with other consciousnesses, we can conceive of knowledge in terms of a subject contemplating the objects it knows about. On the other hand, if our consciousness is itself brought into being by borrowing meanings from the big Other, and if the world *as we know it* owes its differences to language, we can no longer think in terms of a binary opposition between a knowing subject in here and the objects of its knowledge out there.

Truth and knowledge exist at the level of the signifier. In other words, truth is a matter of what we can say (or write, or indicate in diagrams or chemical symbols). If we lay claim to the truth, whether we conceive of this as objective or subjective, we are drawing on the big Other to do so. We are defining what we believe, that is to say, in terms drawn from out there, however much we seem to feel it in here.

To that extent, what we believe is no longer purely personal, but a conviction that culture permits (even if that same culture also deplores it). How many of the beliefs we experience as 'subjective' are in practice culturally instilled?

Relativism instead?

At the same time, however, it does not follow that truth is relative or that all beliefs are equal. What exists does not depend on what we can say exists and poststructuralism does not do away with evidence or argument. There is no plausible case for supposing the earth is flat. On the contrary, such error can be ruled out by counter-evidence without appealing to an opposing truth. People can be mistaken, misled, or misinformed and the moon is not convincingly held to be made of green cheese. The implication of Saussure's insight is not the multiplication of truths but the acknowledgement of doubt.

In consequence, fake news is no less fake than it ever was. Indeed, sometimes the world strikes back against false claims, as I shall argue in Chapter 5. Still less does poststructuralism legitimize lying: while truth is hard to be sure of, it does not follow that it's acceptable to make things up or affirm what you know to be fictitious. People lie to get what they want. Unscrupulous political leaders lie to win power and sometimes their followers agree to be fooled, if that produces the outcomes they prefer. Disinformation is widespread—and easily promoted on social media—but poststructuralism plays no part in licensing dishonesty.

Deconstruction

To recapitulate, poststructuralism claims that the conventional antithesis between subjective and objective doesn't hold, because the subject is produced outside itself. It does not make sense to isolate the subjective, since the subject originates nothing, and we cannot, therefore, appeal to the subject as the absolute origin of its own views. Views are learnt from somewhere, even if we cannot remember where or when, and even if we are the very first person to bring together separate views to make a new one. At the same time, there is no purely objective knowledge, because knowledge is necessarily the property of a subject. A fact may exist forever, even if the human race dies out, but knowledge of it doesn't continue without a subject there to do the knowing. Subjectivity is constituted from outside itself; the objectivity of knowledge is invaded by the knowing subject.

And if you've followed that argument this far, you have just carried out the process that Jacques Derrida identifies as deconstruction, the inevitable intrusion of the other into the selfsame.

The work that first made Derrida's international reputation was *Of Grammatology*, which appeared in French in 1967. The topic, writing, appeared uncontroversial and the title scarcely seemed to herald a blockbuster. And yet *Of Grammatology* delivered a resounding challenge to the entire tradition of Western philosophy, and although the book has been endlessly misread, misquoted, and denounced, its arguments have not so far been effectively refuted.

Jacques Derrida, 1930–2004

Born in Algeria, Derrida moved to Paris at 19 to complete his education. There he taught successively at the Sorbonne, the École Normale Supérieure, and the École des Hautes Études en Sciences Sociales. He was also Professor of Philosophy and Comparative Literature at the University of California, Irvine.

His first book was on Husserl's geometry (1962), but *Of Grammatology*, *Speech and Phenomena*, and *Writing and Difference* were all published in French in 1967. In later works he discussed art, ethics, and politics, experimenting with typography and finding inventive ways to break with linear prose. Of his many books, my personal favourite is probably *The Post Card: From Socrates to Freud and Beyond* (1980), a love story, told in letters (or on very large postcards!), in which the object of a forbidden, impossible desire, it finally turns out, is (probably) the presence promised by metaphysics.

Binary oppositions

Western culture, Derrida argues, depends on binary oppositions. In this respect, structuralists who saw them as foundational were heirs to 25 centuries of thought. Moreover, these oppositions are always hierarchic. One term is highly valued, the other found wanting. Darkness is the absence of light; nature is privileged over culture, just as speech is valued at the expense of writing. But these terms can never sustain the antithesis on which they depend. The meaning of each depends on the trace of the other that inhabits its definition.

Deconstructing Lévi-Strauss

For example, *Of Grammatology* includes a close reading of Lévi-Strauss. In *Tristes Tropiques* Lévi-Strauss recounted what he called 'A Writing Lesson'. The Nambikwara tribe watched the anthropologist making notes and attributed power to the process of writing. When Lévi-Strauss gave them paper and pencils, the Nambikwara soon learned to make wavy lines on the page, presumably in imitation of the practice they had witnessed. But their Chief saw an additional possibility here. With a view to impressing upon his own people his participation in the secrets of the white man, he pretended to read out his own scribbles.

The episode prompts Lévi-Strauss to reflect on the implications of literacy. In accordance with the Western tradition of opposing writing to speech, its secondary transcription, and thus 'fallen' from the natural grace of the purely oral, Lévi-Strauss aligns writing with exploitation and violence. The ethnologist blames himself for destroying the innocent culture of the Nambikwara, and introducing power relations into their communitarian way of life.

Derrida's book is designed to contest the alignment of writing with a fall from nature. On the basis of Lévi-Strauss's own account, and without invoking any exterior information, Derrida shows that the Nambikwara are by no means as innocent as the story would have us believe. For instance, although their culture forbids the use of proper names, when the children quarrel, they betray the names of their antagonists to the anthropologist himself, who then has very little difficulty in extracting the names of everyone else. Violence, perfidy, and the willingness to oppress are already there, even among the children. Writing did not corrupt the Nambikwara: their innocence was imaginary, an anthropologist's dream of a purity lost to the West but still present elsewhere, in a society closer to nature.

Lévi-Strauss has reversed Western ethnocentric values in their conventional form. Instead of despising the Nambikwara, he idealizes them. But because his reversal of values stays within the same theoretical framework of oppositions between nature and culture, speech and writing, it simply reproduces in another mode the ethnocentrism it was designed to challenge.

Derrida's project, however, is not to reverse the hierarchy, to privilege writing over speech. Instead, it is to demonstrate that the valued term, speech, is not exempt from the negative qualities attributed to writing. The 'proper' names of the Nambikwara, he argues, do not belong to individuals as if they were their 'property', the unique name denominating a unique person. On the contrary, names differentiate and classify, just like language—and just like writing.

Derrida's real target here is not the Nambikwara. Nor is it Lévi-Strauss or his anthropology, but what Derrida calls *phonocentrism*, the attribution to the human voice of a presence, an immediacy and a naturalness that is lost in writing. This, he urges, leads to the sentimentalization of a purity and innocence that never was: the oral community, all its members within earshot of each other, *authentic, present to itself.*

Deconstructing Saussure

Saussure himself, Derrida points out on the basis of an equally attentive deconstruction of the *Course in General Linguistics*, was as prone to phonocentrism as Lévi-Strauss—not surprisingly, since Saussure was heir to exactly the same Western philosophical tradition. Linguistics gives primacy to speech. In line with their Western heritage, many specialists in linguistics still see writing as secondary, the inadequate transcription of oral exchange. Saussure's *Course*, Derrida demonstrates, denounces writing as variously unnatural, perverse, monstrous, sinful, tyrannical, pathological.

These are strong terms, and the inference must be that they betray a sense that something important is threatened by the existence of writing. But what?

Writing, Derrida explains, continues to signify in the absence of the writer. If he was an individual at all, Homer was probably present to deliver his poems orally to an audience that recognized the heroic values they endorsed. Thanks to writing, however, we can still read his epics, even though Homer and his first audiences have been dead for nearly 3,000 years. An understanding of the *Odyssey* doesn't depend on our direct access to the fantasy world that Homer described, nor on the presence of Homer himself to confirm that we have understood his *true* meaning.

Of course, in his absence, we have no access to the meaning Homer may have intended to insert into the *Odyssey*. If, ignoring 'The Death of the Author', we identified the true meaning exclusively with Homer's intention, it would follow that we could not now read the *Odyssey* at all. But in practice, we self-evidently *can* follow the story of Odysseus' adventures, imagine the magical world he inhabits, and care about what happens when he finally finds his way home. However anachronistically, we do make some sense of this ancient epic. Writing, therefore, demonstrates that sense may be made in the absence of the author, or at a distance from the *cogito* of consciousness, supposedly present to itself in thought, and uttered (outered, expressed) in the immediacy of unfallen speech.

In this way writing threatens the traditional Western *logocentric* assumption that only speech bears true witness to thought. Logocentrism puts meaning at the centre, imagines that the signified exists in some realm of pure consciousness, and then finds its way out into speech, while writing is no more than the record of what was spoken. Saussure's phonocentrism and his logocentrism, learnt from the culture he inhabits, contradict the radical possibilities of his argument that meaning is an effect of the signifier, that the priority belongs to language itself.

If there are no pure, free-standing meanings, we look in vain, Derrida maintains, for the transcendental signified, the one true meaning that holds all the others in place, the foundational truth that exists beyond question and provides the answer to all subsidiary problems. Metaphysical systems of belief, laying claim to the truth, appeal to a transcendental signified. For Christianity this is God, for the Enlightenment reason, and for science the laws of nature. But if we take meaning to be the effect of language, not its cause, these foundations lose their transcendental status. This does not reduce belief to the status of fiction, but it does undermine its anchorage in a truth beyond question.

In consequence, absolute truth is no longer available as a source of authority. It does not follow that rockets do not reach the moon, or that bridges may suddenly fall down. (They might, but only if the calculations were wrong in the first place.) It simply implies a certain humility in relation to the reasoning that put them there. A good deal of science is hypothetical, rather than certain; some medicine works without our knowing for sure why it does so. Success in practice does not always prove the accuracy of our theoretical map.

Reading Derrida

Q. Derrida is very hard to read. Why doesn't he write more simply? Doesn't he want to communicate?

A. There are three reasons why we have difficulty in reading Derrida. The first is that he is a (Continental) philosopher, with a range of reference that is not widely available outside that tradition. Many of his more impenetrable remarks turn out to be allusions to Plato, Hegel, or Heidegger, and not obscure at all to people who have those writers at their fingertips, in a way that most of us don't. Second, he is very meticulous. What can seem repetitive and precious comes from a desire to be precise. But third, it is also important from the point of view of the case against logocentrism to demonstrate in practice that language is not a window onto ideas in their pure intelligibility. In *Glas*, for example, he unsettles the seeming transparency of linear prose (see Figure 5).

Once again, subjectivity is not an alternative. My personal beliefs are no guarantee of accuracy either. I might believe I could jump off tall buildings and fly—and I should probably find, rather late in the day, I was wrong. What is called into question is not whether we can fly but access to a truth beyond language as the ground of certainty.

Deconstruction, not critique

Traditional Western metaphysics advances on the basis of critique. You find the weakness in your antagonist's argument, and by this means show it to be false. In the tradition of Pope and Swift, you may then ridicule it, lining up your reader for you and against your antagonist. You go on to replace the previous position with your own views, which are then subject to critique in their turn.

what, after all, of the remain(s), today, for us, here, now, of a Hegel?

For us, here, now: from now on that is what one will not have been able to think without him.

For us, here, now: these words are citations, already, always, we will have learned that from him.

Who, him?

His name is so strange. From the eagle it draws imperial or historic power. Those who still pronounce his name like the French (there are some) are ludicrous only up to a certain point: the restitution (semantically infallible for those who have read him a little—but only a little) of magisterial coldness and imperturbable seriousness, the eagle caught in ice and frost, glass and gel.

Let the emblanched [*emblémi*] philosopher be so congealed.

Who, him? The lead or gold, white or black eagle has not signed the text of *savoir absolu*, absolute knowledge. Even less has the red eagle. Besides, whether *Sa* is a text, has given rise to a text, whether it has been written or has written, caused writing, let writing come about is not yet known.

> So from now on *will be the siglum of *savoir absolu*. And IC, let's note this already since the two staffs represent each other, the Immaculate Conception. A properly singular tachygraphy: it is not first going to dislocate, as could be thought, a code, i.e., what we depend [*table*] on too much. But perhaps, much later and more slowly this time, to exhibit its borders*

Whether it lets itself be assigned [*enseigner*], signed, ensigned is not yet known. Perhaps there is an incompatibility (rather than a dialectical contradiction) between the teaching and the signature, a schoolmaster and a signer. Perhaps, in any case, even when they let themselves be thought and signed, these two operations cannot overlap each other [*se recouper*].

> remain(s) to be thought: it (*ça*) does not accentuate itself here now but will already have been put to the test on the other side. Sense must conform, more or less, to the calcul of what the engraver terms a counterproof

Its/His [*Sa*] signature, as thought of the remain(s), will envelop this corpus, but no doubt will not be contained therein.

This is—a legend.

Not a fable: a legend. Not a novel, not a family romance since that concerns Hegel's family, but a legend.

The legend does not pretend to afford a reading of Hegel's whole corpus, texts, and plans [*desseins*], just of two figures. More precisely, of two figures in the act of effacing themselves: two passages.

"*what remained of a Rembrandt torn into small, very regular squares and rammed down the shithole*" is divided in two.

As the remain(s) [*reste*].

Two unequal columns, they say distyle [*disent-ils*], each of which — envelop(e)(s) or sheath(es), incalculably reverses, turns inside out, replaces, remarks, overlaps [*recoupe*] the other.

The incalculable of *what remained* calculates itself, elaborates all the *coups* [strokes, blows, etc.], twists or scaffolds them in silence, you would wear yourself out even faster by counting them. Each little square is delimited, each column rises with an impassive self-sufficiency, and yet the element of contagion, the infinite circulation of general equivalence relates each sentence, each stump of writing (for example, "*je m'éc . . .*") to each other, within each column and from one column to the other of *what remained* infinitely calculable.

Almost.

Of the remain(s), after all, there are, always, overlapping each other, two functions.

The first assures, guards, assimilates, interiorizes, idealizes, relieves the fall [*chute*] into the monument. There the fall maintains, embalms, and mummifies itself, monumemorizes and names itself—falls (to the tomb(stone)) [*tombe*]. Therefore, but as a fall, it erects itself there.

1

Difference or truth?

5. Derrida rejects the illusion of transparency in *Glas*.

Deconstruction, however, is not critique. Derrida treats Lévi-Strauss with respect, and his project is not to persuade us to repudiate Saussure, still less to ridicule him (though there are moments of arcane comedy in his account of the sermon against the sin of writing delivered by the moralist from Geneva). Instead, he points out that Saussure's own book does not sustain the opposition between speech and writing it takes for granted and reiterates. On the contrary, the *Course* records (as an outrage) the invasion of the rejected writing into speech itself. Spelling, Saussure declares with horror, is changing pronunciation.

It does. Modern English examples include the introduction of a pronounced 't' into 'often', which formerly rhymed with 'soften', and the widespread pronunciation of 'again' to rhyme with 'Spain', when it once rhymed with 'then'. Does 'ate' rhyme with 'pet' or 'pate'? It may depend on the age of the speaker. Speech is repeatedly modified by writing: the other invades the selfsame. Neither speech nor writing has logical priority: the two are not antithetical; in literate cultures we learn to signify from both.

Sonnet 18

Shakespeare's Sonnet 18, 'Shall I compare thee to a summer's day?' is one of his most popular poems. People read it out at weddings (though not as often as Sonnet 116) in lyrical celebration of an ideal romance. Will writes it for Viola in John Madden's film *Shakespeare in Love*.

The poem seems to turn on a binary comparison between the beloved and the summer's day, in which the beloved is always the privileged term: 'Thou art more lovely and more temperate.' By contrast with the loved one, the weather is never quite right: 'Rough winds do shake the darling buds of May'; the temperature is either too hot or too cold. Besides, the products of the season are perfect only for a moment, while 'Thy eternal summer shall not fade.'

But what is the condition of this timeless perfection? Writing! The beloved is immune to decline and death only 'When in eternal lines to time thou grow'st'. These lines of verse, it turns out, are what endows the mortal human being with immortality: 'So long as men can breathe, or eyes can see, | So long lives this, and this gives life to thee.' 'This', Sonnet 18, in other words, celebrates its own power to confer eternity.

The binary opposition, then, is not quite as simple as it first appeared. 'Thou' and the summer day, distinguished as antithetical, now appear on the same side of a line that divides mortality from poetry. All that lives is transitory, including the beloved: 'Every fair from fair sometime declines.' Just like the summer day, the living object of the poet's desire will, after all, fade and die. Immortality belongs only to the poem and the poem's inscription of love.

But if love and summer resemble one another after all, in contrast to writing, which alone has immortal powers, what are we to make of the excess heat and cold of the summer day? Are they also properties the season shares with human love? Does the Sonnet imply that love too is very rarely, in practice, just right? And the rough winds that shake the darling buds? Are they, perhaps, tempestuous, the element of passion that makes love itself anything but 'temperate'?

The other invades the selfsame. The qualities of the repudiated summer day return to inhabit the romance they seemed designed to define by contrast.

What exactly, then, does Sonnet 18 claim? You are better than a summer's day, since you won't fade now that I've written this poem? Or, alternatively, you are mortal, like a summer's day, and won't fade if—and only if—I immortalize you in my poem? Who is in control here, the 'lovely' but mutable object of desire, or the desiring but life-giving poet? Or is the Sonnet a dramatization of a miniature power struggle, the sequence of implied threats and promises that goes on just below the surface of so many passionate relationships? Exactly how idealistic *is* this lyrical text? What is the *truth* of Sonnet 18? Perhaps it's undecidable?

Différance

Arguably, that element of undecidability, so common in Shakespeare's plays as well as the Sonnets, and the deferral by the signifier of a single, determinable thematic meaning, or logos, plays a part in the continuing fascination of his work for us now, four centuries after its composition.

Derrida examines the implications of what survives in Saussure's work if we take out the logocentrism implied by his phonocentrism, the residual privilege he accords to ideas and the voice. Meaning, Derrida concludes, is always the effect of the *trace* of the other in the selfsame.

How do we define nature? Not by reference to flowers and trees, probably, since they are found in parks, and can be cultivated, but as wildness, the absence of culture. By reference, in other words, to the term that is excluded by and from nature itself. And yet it is precisely from within culture that we are able to identify nature at all. The one term cannot be excluded from the meaning of the other. Meaning depends on difference.

It also, Derrida proposes, invokes differance (with an *a*). If the signifier *differs* from another signifier, it also *defers* the meaning it produces. (English cannot capture the French pun or homonym: *différer* is both to differ and to defer.) That is to say, the signifier eclipses the signified. Logocentrism imagines there is a pure concept, an idea. But where is this to be found? The signifier takes its place. Only the signifier is present in writing or speech: the imagined presence of the meaning as pure idea is deferred, pushed away, and postponed, relegated by the signifier, which is all we can bring before us, or isolate for inspection.

Differance, a process, not an action we perform or undergo, neither active nor passive (like other terms ending in 'ance': assistance, resonance), is the only source of meaning. But differance has no content; it does not name any kind of presence or transcendence. It is not a concept. Indeed, it is not even a word.

In his essay on 'Differance', Derrida demonstrates that the term he has invented on the basis of the French homonym is both an instance of deconstruction and an ironic tribute to Saussure. It is impossible in speech, he reiterates, to use the term without explicitly invoking the spelling. You cannot *hear* the difference between 'difference' and 'differance' (or *différence* and *différance*). The only way to make the distinction evident in speech is to say 'differance (with an *a*)'. Writing is triumphantly shown to invade the act of speaking. (Unfortunately, one of Derrida's translators left the word in 'French'. His English-speaking admirers miss the point, however, when they deliver the word as if it were French, or in an imitation of French pronunciation.)

Differance, neither a signifier (until Derrida coined it) nor a signified (since it conjures up no imagined presence), is, nevertheless, the only origin of meaning. Not *full* (of an idea), nor *empty* (since it is intelligible), not foundational, since it cannot be appealed to as a guarantee of truth, differance is, all the same, what enables us to understand each other—to the degree that we do.

The strange case of Richard Mutt

What are the implications of all this? How, in practice, does deconstruction affect our understanding of the world?

In April 1917 the American Society of Independent Artists held an exhibition. Modernism was in full swing, and this radical group was determined not to allow conventional values to determine what counted as art. The slogan for the exhibition was 'No jury, no prizes'. In order to avoid even the most unintended hierarchy, Marcel Duchamp, an influential member of the Independents, is said to have suggested that the works should be hung in alphabetical order, starting with a letter drawn from a hat. For this inventive idea he was elected Chair of the hanging committee.

The Independents drew the line, however, at an entry submitted by Richard Mutt, a readymade urinal, turned on its side and named *Fountain*. *Fountain* was not shown and, in defence of artistic freedom, Duchamp promptly resigned his place on the committee. The following month, the second issue of Duchamp's journal *The Blind Man* carried an unsigned editorial defending *Fountain*, and the cover showed a picture of the object itself by Alfred Stieglitz, the prestigious New York photographer and gallery-owner. The photo reveals an elegantly shadowed but clearly recognizable upturned urinal, signed 'R. Mutt 1917'.

As is now well known, R. Mutt was Marcel Duchamp, and *Fountain* was to become one of the most highly prized works of the 20th century. All that remains of the original, which was never shown, is the photograph, signifier of a signifier, the image of a 'work' that involved no work at all, by an artist who did not exist. Much later, Duchamp authorized a number of 'copies', now displayed in Paris, London, New York, and elsewhere (see Figure 6). As readymades, the copies were not exact replicas of the first *Fountain*, or each other. The lost original is infinitely deferred, supplanted by the copies. Tate Modern displays a version of 1964, and a facsimile of *The Blind Man* is also on show in a glass case.

Thierry de Duve has argued that Duchamp's work in general, and *Fountain* in particular, mark a turning-point in aesthetics. Duchamp's readymades call into question the definition of art. Was it art, this object which could hardly be described as beautiful, at least by conventional standards? Was it art, if it could be bought readymade, and required no skill to produce? Was it art if it rejected all notion of expression or creativity? And finally, was it art if, as the work of a painter, it repudiated both paint and canvas, and yet, while standing firm in three dimensions, bore no other resemblance to existing sculpture either?

In 1917 the American Society of Independent Artists said no. But two generations later the art world resoundingly said yes, and there are copies of *Fountain* all over the world.

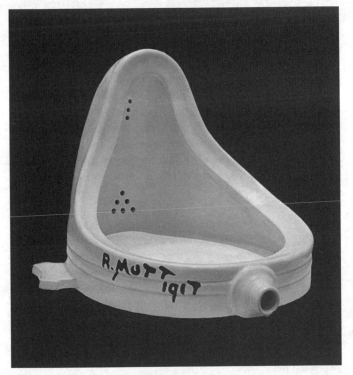

6. Is it art? Marcel Duchamp's *Fountain*.

Who was right? Is there a correct answer? Not really: the question is probably undecidable, since the definition of art is not subject to legislation. Is the decision 'subjective', then? You can make up your own mind.

Yet in practice, however personal and individual it may feel, your choice depends on meaning, which is not subjective, but conventional, and the condition of subjectivity itself. If you define art in terms of beauty, skill, or creativity, your answer has to be no; if you define it as what the art world calls art, or what the artist decides to call art, or what *anyone* chooses to call art, your answer must be yes.

So the question is linguistic, and the debates about what constitutes art are in the end debates about language. Who defines terms? Who has the right to decide what they mean? Can anyone finally and definitively say what art *is*? Poststructuralism would say not. The meaning, the concept, the truth of art is always differed and deferred by the signifier. 'Art' as pure idea cannot be made present to consciousness. *Fountain* both poses the question and stands in the way of any final, indisputable answer.

It is no solution, then, to argue that *Fountain* strips the signifier 'art' of all meaning. On the contrary, the word continues to mean, even if it means differently. For those who include *Fountain* in the category of art, the meaning of the term is irreversibly changed. Non-art (the readymade, the urinal) invades art (creative and uplifting); the trace of the other appears in the selfsame; and from then on, at least, the meaning of art has become undecidable. Art is no longer a pure concept we can appeal to in order to judge Andy Warhol's *Brillo Boxes* or Tracey Emin's *Bed*. But then, perhaps it never was.

The implications of undecidability

Saussure's diagrams of the sign as a self-contained oval, with a line across the middle dividing signifier from signified, might give the impression that each signifier brings with it its own inseparable, single meaning. Deconstruction undoes that impression, pushes meaning towards undecidability, and in the process democratizes language. Binary oppositions do not hold: they can always be undone. The trace of otherness in the selfsame lays all oppositions open to deconstruction, leaving no pure or absolute concepts that can be taken as foundational. Meanings, not only the meaning of 'art' but that of 'democracy' itself, or 'terrorism', or 'human rights', for example, are not individual, personal, or subjective, since they emanate from language. But they are not given in nature, or guaranteed by any existing authority either.

At the same time, meanings are lived. Art fetches high prices, democracy is invoked to justify wars, and terrorists are hunted down. Human rights are a utopian aspiration and not, in most parts of the world, a reality. But they motivate legally binding decisions.

If meanings are not given or guaranteed, but lived all the same, it follows that they can be challenged and changed. And this is so not just for authority figures. If meaning is a matter of social convention, it concerns and involves all of us.

Chapter 5
Difference in the world

Where in all this talk of meaning is the actuality of the world? A familiar objection to poststructuralism is that it privileges words over things. Detractors pounce gleefully on Derrida's hostage to fortune in *Of Grammatology*, translated as '*There is nothing outside of the text*' [*il n'y a pas de hors-texte*]. 'So deconstruction does disavow the world, after all,' they gloat. 'Poststructuralists are saying that materiality doesn't exist outside our own heads. Any statements about the world are as valid as any others and, deny it as you will, poststructuralism is complicit with the post-truth age of lies, fake news, and alternative facts.'

In practice, however, the material world exercises determinations that language struggles to accommodate. Poststructuralists are more likely to see symbolization as inadequate than all-encompassing. Understood in context, Derrida's statement doesn't deny the world, or claim that nothing exists but textuality. Instead, it points to the limitations of texts. They cannot make present what they only represent or stand in for, but only subject it to differance (with an *a*).

The passage in question concerns reading. In a chapter headed '…That Dangerous Supplement…' Derrida puts forward an interpretation of Jean-Jacques Rousseau's *Confessions*, taking advantage in the process of an ambiguity not available in English.

Suppléer means to compensate for a lack, to replace, as well as to add. Rousseau's book, Derrida argues, shows presence repeatedly eclipsed by the substitutions and supplements called on to compensate for its loss. Each attempt to reappropriate the lost presence only distances it further.

In the process of making the case, he defines reading as more than paraphrase. Readings are made; the act of reading is to be understood as a task; his own reading is produced by work performed on the text. Rousseau's *Confessions* concerns his personal behaviour and intimate relationships. The book inevitably solicits the kind of interpretation that bypasses the words to find a free-standing signified or a referential content, a state of mind, the author's psychobiography.

But, as Derrida has consistently argued, meaning cannot be brought before us in its pure state, since the signified content is always deferred, relegated by the signifier. The signifier, which looks supplementary, a *re*-presentation of an idea, in practice replaces the signified. That substitute, masquerading as an addition, is all we have. Jean-Jacques's psychological state cannot be made present by Rousseau's writing.

And this is not only, Derrida goes on, because we have no access, apart from the text, to the author's close relationships. A productive reading traces in Rousseau's text itself something of greater interest to deconstruction, an account of one substitution after another that is also an accretion. Jean-Jacques never knew the mother who died giving birth to him, *The Confessions* records. Each new character in the story will seem not only to make up for her loss but to offer something extra in the process. Mme de Warens, 'Mamma', more than stands in for his lost mother. His sexual partner Thérèse will explicitly more than stand in for Mamma. And masturbation more than stands in for sex, since it places all women at Jean-Jacques's disposal. But something—the longed-for restitution of presence, of undifferentiated plenitude—eludes him in each of these instances.

What goes for the characters here also goes for the relationship between speech and writing. Rousseau, an ardent phonocentrist, convinced that writing is artificial, no more than a substitute for and adjunct to the naturalness of speech, writes, even so, he affirms, because in company shyness makes him speak foolishly; he cannot make himself present in the conversation as he truly is. But what Jean-Jacques perceives as a personal problem holds for all speech. When interiority annexes the signifier to take outward form, it necessarily dispossesses the subject it also constitutes, and writing is called on to fill the gap. This further adjunct is called on to compensate for the inadequacy of the spoken word but, as an addition, yet again relegates the missing presence it is required to restore.

As Derrida will go on to put it, 'The re-presentation is also a de-presentation.' Supplementarity as addition and substitution at once defines textuality and banishes presence. The need for a supplement brought in from outside exposes a deficiency—and an impossibility, since the supplement too is deficient, unable to perform the task expected of it. Meaning cannot be made present in writing or speech and there is no unmediated access to idea or actuality. And yet meaning exists nowhere but in the signifier: the outside finds its only intelligible place there.

Rousseau's written text, like all texts, is able to signify in the absence of the author, represents him, and so supplants his actual presence. There is nothing outside the text we can call on to make up for that absence. What is more, *The Confessions* includes no supplementary *hors-texte* we can appeal to for evidence of Jean-Jacques's state of mind—and Derrida here puns on the *hors-texte* as extra material, especially the plates or engravings in a book that seem to provide an alternative way of recovering its truth. All we have is Rousseau's text as supplement to and substitute for its own supposed content. But, productively read, the text unwittingly reveals that writing is no more than another name for differance. By this means, it adds to what its author knows, and so more than stands in for psychobiography.

Mastery in question

We might also note that Derrida's interpretation of *The Confessions* itself supplements the work, acting as both addition and substitute. His reading finds the blind spot in a book that belongs to a language and a cultural moment its author can never fully dominate. Accompanying the text as a guide, this rereading—or rewriting—deepens the work it also stands in for, with the effect of bringing to light its prevision of differance.

But what is the status of Derrida's reading? Doesn't it claim to have uncovered the truth of deconstruction foreshadowed by Rousseau's text? If so, '…That Dangerous Supplement…' does no more than follow the traditional practice of the history of philosophy as Sarah Kofman defines it: a form of mastery that uncovers in past works anticipations of current thinking.

In her book *Freud and Fiction*, Kofman herself reads four of Freud's own readings of works of art, where the founder of psychoanalysis finds his own insights foreseen and therefore confirmed. In the process, they are elevated to the status of universality. But, she insists, Freud's supplementary reduction of a text to a single, decipherable, timeless meaning is illegitimate, dangerous. His readings, she points out, are blind to details that do not corroborate his theory.

The difference poststructuralism makes is that, in explicitly producing an interpretation, it acknowledges that every reading is located at a specific cultural moment. All interpretation belongs to a language and time its author cannot fully command and is subject, in consequence, to its own blindnesses. Where traditional philosophy claims to see clearly what was previously obscure, poststructuralism forgoes such hopes of perfect mastery.

Nothing in Derrida's discussion of reading implies that the world does not exist or that there is only the signifier. His case concerns not what exists but the inability of the text to provide access to what lies outside it. Names intervene between us and things, leaving knowledge open to doubt; interpretation is subject to blindnesses, as well as interests and motivations. But that does not legitimate disinformation, or the wilful dissemination of falsehoods. On the contrary. Lies are not acknowledgements of uncertainty but claims to know something we don't; in short, ungrounded bids for mastery.

The desire for presence

The naming that relegates ideas and actuality does not do away with a longing for presence, for unconditional knowledge. In fantasy, we erase the signifier to secure direct access to meaning and the world. According to Jacques Lacan's adaptation of Freud, it is the *Non* of prohibition that generates the longing for what it rules out. And in Derrida's adaptation of Lacan, differance produces not only the distinction between presence and absence but also the appetite for what it forbids:

> Without the possibility of differance, the desire of presence as such would not find its wind.... Differance produces what it interdicts, makes possible the very thing that it makes impossible.

Rousseau's *Confessions* records an ungratified longing. A wanderer, driven from place to place across Europe in search of a refuge where he can be at one with his beloved nature, Jean-Jacques never manages to settle or find contentment, Rousseau records. Later, *The Post Card*, Derrida's love story, does not name the object of desire, the one who always maintains an unbridgeable distance. But as I read the book, her (or his or its) designation is presence.

The Post Card was first published in French in 1980. At a conference I attended in Glasgow in 1986, Derrida was asked what he had against presence. I vividly remember his reply, as he spread his arms in a shrug that was simultaneously an embrace: 'I have nothing against it! It would be wonderful. But you would be dead.' Oddly enough, the written record of the proceedings does not include this exchange. Instead, a more laborious question elicits a more ponderous response from Derrida:

> my desire, for good, for presence, my own metaphysics of presence, not only cannot be accomplished, meets its limit, but *should* not be accomplished because the accomplishment or the fulfilment of this desire for presence would be death itself; the good, the absolute good, would be identical with death.

The written record claims to be 'minimally-edited'. Have I imagined my recollection, sharp and clear though it is? I'd love to know but I can't be sure—can't, in other words, make that past moment unequivocally present to my consciousness.

The world strikes back

What then, in the light of all this, is the relationship between language and the world? Signifying creatures as we are, we cannot find a secure basis for knowledge independent of signification. And yet, while language constrains our thinking, it does not command the external world. Instead, whether or not we acknowledge it, the world of things exercises its own determinations. Climate-change denial, for instance, does not stop species migrating, the glaciers melting, or sea levels rising. If global warming goes unchecked, it stands to remake the land masses of the planet. Coastal cities will be flooded; the frozen

Conflicts of interest

Q. Freak weather events—droughts, forest fires, floods, hurricanes—are increasing. World temperatures are rising and the ice caps are shrinking. Isn't this evidence that we know what goes on outside our signifying systems?

A. If we know, that is because the climate emergency is repeatedly measured, named, and blamed in lectures, news bulletins, books, films, and cartoons, to the point where denial is perverse—or motivated. The problem is not knowledge but conflicts of interest. The fossil-fuel industry wants things to go on as before, while nations postpone action that might limit economic growth by bickering over who should take responsibility for change (see Figure 7).

7. Chappatte, *Carbon Footprint*. Conflicts of interest prolong the emergency.

north will become subject to cultivation, while the south will be desert. The need to reduce the use of fossil fuels means that no more of the globe can safely be globalized. Whole populations will crowd into the available spaces and recourse to nationalism, with ever-stronger borders, will not in the end keep out migrants.

Making decisions

But if we can't be certain, even so, of the facts, how can we decide what course to take? In this instance, we know about climate change from the science that explains the events we experience or watch on TV. That knowledge has no guarantees outside the scientific arguments themselves and there is no appeal to a still higher, independent authority, no science of the science. Even so, individuals decide whether or not to act on the basis of the information available. Either course has effects, however minor, on individual behaviour and the world.

French philosophy develops in the (often silent) awareness of Pascal's wager. Pascal argued that, if God exists, eternal life is at stake, and faithful obedience stands to win immortality. Conversely, if God is a fiction, believers won't have lost much that was truly precious. Arguably, if the climate emergency exists, life on the planet is at stake; if it doesn't, the switch to renewables won't have done much harm—except to the fossil-fuel corporations.

We have no choice but to act in the world, although without the assurance that certainty would provide. Paradoxically, inaction also counts as action in that it leaves things as they are. Although poststructuralism withholds confirmation of truth from the other side of the signifier, it has no place for the rationalization of apathy.

The event

The world affirms its existence in the *event*, a term that resonates through much poststructuralist writing. In a specialized sense, an event, experienced as a rupture, has unforeseen repercussions, not least for the language that sets out to represent it. Existing vocabularies cannot do it justice. The formative events of May 1968 (*Les Événements de mai*), when students and unions took possession of the streets of Paris, were bound to evoke the decisive event of the French Revolution. The revolt against privilege in 1789–93 defined new rights—and wrongs. In the process it changed the vocabulary as well as the practice of politics.

On 11 September 2001, hijacked airliners destroyed the World Trade Center in New York. We watched the TV pictures again and again, mostly in silence. What could we say? To many viewers it felt unreal, the nearest available comparison a fictional disaster movie. The event was nameable only by its date, 9/11. And then, within days, a new phrase emerged in America. 'The war on terror' would in due course realign East and West both practically and ideologically.

Pandemics are events. At the time I write, the outcomes of Covid-19, medical, economic, and social, remain unknown. At the very least, the convulsion has thrown into relief the thinness of the fabrics that sustain communities, local, national, and international.

But, as the most shocking event of the 20th century—and indeed of all history—it was the holocaust that pervaded political and philosophical discussion in the post-war period, when poststructuralism was in the making. What vocabulary could match this mass extermination? How could the existing modes of representation do justice to the crimes committed when innocent communities were systematically deported, humiliated, tortured, and killed? The enormity of the event defies the conventions of political and philosophical debate, not to mention everyday exchange. This wrong 'is not presentable', argues Jean-François Lyotard in *The Differend*, 'under the rules of knowledge'.

Sarah Kofman's *Smothered Words* is dedicated to the memory of her father, who died in Auschwitz. The book begins with epigraphs from Maurice Blanchot. 'The holocaust, the *absolute* event of history...How can it be preserved, even by thought?' 'The wish of all, in the camps, the last wish: know what has happened, do not forget, and at the same time you will never know.' The injustice cannot be made present to anyone who wasn't there.

Borrowing from Derrida's account of differance, Kofman calls Auschwitz, 'neither a concept nor a pure name'. Instead, it remains 'a name beyond naming'. (Derrida borrows back the parallel to discuss the holocaust in *For What Tomorrow*.) Kofman records

Sarah Kofman, 1934–94

Born in Paris to Jewish parents who had left Poland five years earlier. After her father's deportation in 1942, the family spent the rest of the war in hiding. *Rue Ordener, rue Labat* (1994) records Kofman's childhood experiences in the following 10 years, including the wartime imperative to renounce her Jewish identity.

Taught by Deleuze and Derrida, she specialized in the work of Nietzsche and then went on in 1970 to publish a book on Freud's aesthetics, *The Childhood of Art*. Ten years later, *The Enigma of Woman* concerns Freud's writings on female sexuality. In response to a deconstructive reading, Freud's account, Kofman maintains, is more subtle and more sympathetic than contemporary French feminist philosophers allow. But, baffled in his quest for truth by the difficulty of reconciling women's independence with the psychoanalytic theory of castration, Freud eventually lighted on the metaphysical idea of penis envy. This appeased his anxiety but failed to resolve the enigma he faced.

her father's death in dates and figures: the identification numbers as well as the totals of people included in the same convoy, selected for work, or gassed immediately. These severe columns of digits at once testify to the dehumanization of the victims and demonstrate the impossibility of communicating the incommunicable.

Her verbal commemoration shows a similar restraint:

> My father, a rabbi, was killed because he tried to observe the
> Sabbath in the death camps; buried alive with a shovel for
> having—or so the witnesses reported—refused to work on that day,
> in order to celebrate the Sabbath, to pray to God for them all,
> victims and executioners.

Bodies

However far the signifier shapes what we can know for sure, and whatever the limits on what we can name, human beings inhabit the world. And what we do has effects on the world of things and, indeed, bodies. The networks of knowledge that language allows have implications in practice. Foucault's *Discipline and Punish*, for instance, brings together language and bodies without reducing one to the other or privileging either. Each is productive for the other. When in the West corporal punishment and public execution gave way to bodies disciplined by the rules and routines of the prison, a modified vocabulary named new crimes and penalties, classified distinct offences, and codified different degrees of criminal responsibility.

Like the world, however, bodies fought back, when crime persisted and riots showed that prisoners were not always subdued by the regulations designed to control them. Meanwhile, as *The History of Sexuality* affirms, the 19th-century classification of sexual norms and perversions led people to assign new meanings and values to their behaviour. But a regime that subjected erotic practices to the signifier also generated the option of reclaiming the censured pleasures of the body.

The human organism

If we inhabit the world, it also inhabits us. We are not only thinking, speaking subjects but at the same time organisms, constrained by our physiology. The human animal is an assembly of organic materials; the brain relies on neurons and neurotransmitters; mental events are also electro-chemical reactions.

Moods stem from hormones we share with other animals. And some of the most familiar sensations and experiences are inherited from our evolutionary ancestors who, we assume, had no words for them. Jacques Derrida has commented extensively on animals. *The Animal that Therefore I Am*, first published in French in 2006, concerns ethics; *The Beast and the Sovereign* (2008–10) centres on politics. He also proposes that we pay more attention to animal behaviour and especially the work of primatologists. Suppose we do? What we might find are impulses we share with our primate predecessors.

For instance, there is no barrier to control the taxi queue at my local railway station. Instead, enterprising passengers can simply bypass those of us waiting our turn and take the next available cab. In the rush hour, such behaviour regularly elicits rage, amounting to blind fury when it's raining or worse. There are no words that do justice to this condition, experienced physiologically as rising heat, a tensing of the muscles, feelings of aggression towards the opportunist. Of course, as properly socialized citizens, we bear it for a bit, then protest with, 'I hate it when that happens', 'There is a queue, you know.' But what we say is an outlet, not a description of how we feel.

The primatologist Frans de Waal reports an experiment that shows how far the capacity for outrage exists in capuchin monkeys. In the laboratory, two animals are repeatedly rewarded for handing the researcher a stone. At first, both munch happily on their pieces of cucumber. But when one monkey is given a much tastier grape instead, its neighbour has what can only be called a tantrum. The capuchin throws the cucumber back at the researcher, rattles the bars of its cage, and thumps the table bearing the unfair rewards.

We are entitled to recognize something of ourselves here. There are continuities between our reaction and the monkey's to perceived unfairness. Other animal research shows that our evolutionary relatives feel intense emotions, including fear and distress, but also grief and sympathy. Elephants mourn their dead and celebrate family reunions. It is thought that current elephant populations are subject to chronic stress, traumatized by having seen so many of their relatives killed by ivory poachers.

Many creatures protect their young and animals have been found capable of altruistic behaviour, cooperation, and compassion. Rats have been known to free other rats from a trap. Rats also laugh when they are tickled, although the sound is above the frequency we can hear. In one widely visited video, a baby orang-utan laughs uproariously at a simple magic trick.

In my view, while popularizing behavioural biologists draw attention to revealing parallels, they can, like evolutionary psychologists, get carried away by their own enthusiasm. At one moment, they point out that about half of human conduct is determined by evolution; at the next, they may maintain that animals are just like us. But half is not the whole and animals are not quite like us. A major difference is human culture. Although certain animals are not without culture, and can learn from one another to copy new habits, our own customary practices are registered in language. For the taxi queue, culture prescribes certain modes of resistance, while the ability to represent things in their absence enables us to reassure one another that more taxis will arrive in due course. The rules of queuing are themselves cultural—and culturally relative.

Anyone who doubts the way vocabulary shapes allegiances might do worse than correlate popular beliefs with the values promoted in the tabloid newspapers. If the press does not invent these convictions, it encapsulates, legitimates, and so reinforces them. Capuchin monkeys can be made to feel outrage by differential rewards, but not by the rhetorical replacement of the term *compromise* with *surrender*. Animal fake news is possible: some alarm or distress calls are unfounded. But animals don't enlist each other with conspiracy theories, not to mention catchy slogans that simplify complex issues.

Individual species share systems of differences. They make and recognize signals: alarm calls are distinct from mating cries or territorial claims. And, indeed, different alarm calls may indicate distinct threats or degrees of urgency. In other words, animals convey information about existing wants, concerns, dangers. Chimpanzee gestures can mean 'come here' or 'hop on my back'. But human symbolization is able to invoke what is not present, including plans for tomorrow or the merits of alternative options. Syntax can introduce and organize causes, conditions, chronologies.

Thought, deliberation, and argument depend on signification. So far, no one has found evidence of non-human debate, conflicting parties discussing the pros and cons of internationalism, or discussing the rights of self-identifying trans women to access female safe spaces.

Beyond words

Thought implies consciousness as the effect of language. But that leaves a whole area of shared experience where feelings or intuitions find no precise verbal equivalent. Take pain, for instance. How do we describe it, quantify it? In sudden fear we are more likely to gasp or scream than form coherent sentences defining our state of mind. On the TV news mothers weep soundlessly over their children killed in mass shootings. Such emotions, people say, are beyond words—and may be felt all the more intensely in that the conventional idioms don't live up to the feelings. Pain, fear, and grief are among the experiences the little human animal inherits.

Paradoxically, the symbolization that brings us what we know of the world faces limits when it comes to what we feel. Poststructuralism recognizes moments when language fails. Here is Jacques Derrida commenting on Lyotard's death:

> I feel at such a loss, unable to find public words for what is happening to us, for what has left speechless all those who had the good fortune to come near this great thinker.

At funerals, ritual and poetry offer to fill the gap between bereavement and its representation. And yet, consciously or not, Derrida's observation echoes centuries of poetic insistence that mourning defies signification. Hamlet, lamenting the death of his father, wears black, he says; he sighs, weeps, and hangs his head, adopting all the signifiers of grief. But none of this can do justice to 'that within which passes show'. In one of his elegies, John Donne complains: 'Language thou art too narrow, and too weak | To ease us now; great sorrow cannot speak.'

Great love cannot speak either. Even though it goes on trying in romances, lyric poems, pop songs, and Hollywood movies, love has never been definitively delineated. Despite the effort that goes into bypassing the limits of the signifier, the journey always comes back to the same place: it can't be done. What *can* be named are the limits themselves; what can be told is what language *can't* do. And what it can't do is capture romantic love, since love exceeds the Cartesian *cogito*, the consciousness that is constructed in language. Love involves the mind as well as the body; it is both idealizing and visceral.

'I love you more than words can say', the most romantic of affirmations, points to a limit the signifier seems unable to cross. Roland Barthes dwells on the issue in *A Lover's Discourse*:

> the more I experience the speciality of my desire, the less I can name it; to the precision of the target corresponds a quivering of the name; what is proper to desire can produce only an impropriety of the utterance. Of this failure of language, there remains only one trace: the word 'adorable'.

The French resonances of *proper* and *improper* are lost in translation. What is proper to desire, its own, what belongs to it, produces only an inappropriate vocabulary, linguistic error. Language collapses, leaving only a trace of love's intensity in the word 'adorable'.

But *adorable* doesn't do it. *Adorable*, *A Lover's Discourse* continues, is the pointless trace of an exhaustion of language.

> From word to word, I wear myself out to put into other words the selfsameness of my Image, to identify improperly [and inappropriately] what is proper to [and belongs to] my desire.

But, in the end, all that remains is a tautology. '*The adorable is what is adorable*. Or again: I adore you because you are adorable, I love you because I love you.'

Stuttering

What does *adorable* mean? The correct translation of the word, Barthes says, would be the Latin *ipse*, the same, the very person: *c'est lui, c'est bien lui, en personne*. *Adorable*, Barthes says, tries to name the feature that my desire singles out as special. But this quality cannot be located, designated, identified: I shall never, the lover allows, know anything about it: my language will always grope and stutter in the effort to define it.

Gilles Deleuze celebrates a figurative stuttering that marks the moment when language presses outside itself towards creativity. That outside, the outside of language, he insists, not somewhere on the other side of it, is a space to take flight from the relentless battery of information and instruction that signification imposes on us. According to Deleuze, the best writers stutter, straining towards an intensity eloquence cannot reach.

Anyone, he asserts, can rehearse old memories, invent stories, deliver opinions. Some people even acquire style, and can earn a living as celebrated writers. But they dig under the stories, crack open opinions, and reach regions without memories, when they break with convention to go beyond mere fluency. Deleuze favours modernism: e. e. cummings and Samuel Beckett are singled out among others. At the same time, 'To make the language itself stutter in this manner, at the deepest level of style, is a creative process that runs through all great works. It is as if the language were becoming animal.'

Eloquence is subject to its own incompleteness. However hard-won, it remains, paradoxically, too easy, promising a mastery of the world that it cannot be sure to deliver. Poststructuralism is haunted by the limits of language and its theorists pay special attention to the hesitations, the silences, that break up what we say. They can be seen as forms of regression—to our evolutionary heritage or a childhood prior to signification. But this regress is inescapable. If human thought, as Jean-François Lyotard maintains in one of his essays, does not go on without a body, it cannot simply discard its own past.

The real

In an exceptionally untranslatable epigraph to his *Lectures d'enfance*, Lyotard draws attention to the practice of elision, marking the omission that writing so often harbours. In giving this a new name, he relies on the two related meanings of the Latin *infantia*: on the one hand, *speechlessness*, or *lack of eloquence*, and on the other, *babyhood*.

> Let's christen it *infantia*, that which does not speak. An infancy
> that is not a time of life and that does not pass. It haunts discourse.
> Discourse perpetually pushes it into the background…but persists,
> all the same, in constituting it, as lost…If childhood lives on in it,
> that is not *although* but *because* it resides with the adult.

Lyotard here draws silently on Jacques Lacan's account of the real.

The real survives from infancy, when nothing had a name, a condition prior to difference. This infancy-in-the-real is not so much a chronological moment as a retrospective construct. In practice, there's no time when babies are not surrounded by signification, named by others, differentiated, talked to, or spoken of by their doting parents. 'It's a girl!' the midwife might say—although without expecting the new arrival to make much of the announcement.

We cannot discuss or acknowledge the real in the symbolic, except as a theoretical possibility. It belongs to the prehistory of the subject. And yet it lives on in the organism that we continue to be. It does not exist for the subject, the signifying being we become, in the sense that we know nothing about it. In the subject, the real is superseded—but not entirely surmounted. It haunts eloquence in the form of disrupting elisions. A tongue-tied silence—of the kind that inhibited Rousseau in company—may mark its intrusion into discourse.

But although we know nothing about the real, we know about the moment when it begins to be left behind, renounced and replaced by the symbol. In *Beyond the Pleasure Principle* Freud tells how his grandson, Little Ernst, came to terms with the necessary comings and goings of his mother. Both Ernst's mother and his admiring grandfather agreed that the boy had arrived at linguistic difference when he threw away his toy with a childish effort at 'gone' and retrieved it with a triumphant 'there'. The game simulated what Freud calls the child's great cultural achievement, his renunciation of instinctual satisfaction in letting his mother leave without protesting. By signifying her departure in a game and in words, Ernst was able to master his anxiety, Freud proposes.

But Ernst comes to terms with this loss by symbolizing it, by recourse to another mode, a game that represents the event. Representation is always other, belongs to the big Other, the order of language and culture. And when the real is at stake the words, derived from the big Other, don't do it justice, miss it. As Hamlet urges, that within passes show.

In this sense, the mastery the subject achieves is always relative. Little Ernst takes control of his emotions when he names his mother's absence, but that doesn't stop her going away. The loss of the real cannot be repaired by the signifier, and it can be named only by invoking the Otherness of the symbolic order. The real is dead to the subject—or playing dead, gone to ground but liable to stir from time to time in the form of a silence, a stutter, or an allusion to loss.

Mastery revisited

Oddly enough, Little Ernst's story brings into renewed focus the question of mastery, this time in the form posed by Humpty Dumpty: who is in control? Signification allows the child to command his anxiety but not the occurrences that give rise to it.

Moreover, in symbolizing his loss, the little boy renounces the desire to dominate his mother's behaviour: he concedes her freedom. What Lacan calls the symbolic order is a discipline that not only confers advantages. In subscribing to the order of language and culture, the subject cuts the bond with the organism it continues to be and succumbs to the *Non* of prohibition that represses its deepest impulses.

Ernst learns to mean—and to submit. The language that promises us mastery of the world also risks mastering us. If language as Saussure understands it is a prison-house that constrains our thought and conduct, how can we hope to escape its constraints? Change happens, but why?

Poststructuralism takes on the question left unanswered by structuralism. If thinking is determined by structures that escape our awareness, if our account of the world is already scripted by a prevailing wisdom that comes from outside us, how is new thinking possible? How far are we agents of our own future? The ethical and political implications of the poststructuralist analysis of signifying practice are the theme of the final chapter.

Chapter 6
Dissent

A common misreading of poststructuralist theory—that it deprives us of the power to choose—is another instance of binary thinking. If the subject is an effect of meaning, if we are not the free, unconstrained origin of our own beliefs and values, if knowledge can't be relied on, if mastery is an illusion, so the story goes, we cannot regard ourselves as agents in our own lives.

This is not how most poststructuralist thinkers have argued, however. Deconstruction indicates, on the contrary, that meanings, values, and what we (think we) know are all open to pressure for change. Psychoanalysis, meanwhile, sees unconscious desire as defying the values that culture proposes as proper objectives. Foucault also stresses the possibility of resistance—on the basis that power is always authority over something or someone capable of disobeying. (No one, as far as I know, claims sovereignty over turnips.)

In sum, Foucault's model of social relations is unstable, mobile, transferable: the assumptions that reinforce power can be reversed to undermine it. Derrida's philosophy, although it removes certainty, still requires choice and responsibility, ethical and political. Jean-François Lyotard argues against bland consensus. Gilles Deleuze and Alain Badiou, while distancing themselves in some respects from poststructuralism, draw in different ways on its insights to put forward radical views. Both assume that we take sides.

Responsibility

Much of Derrida's later work has been concerned with ethics, the problem of right action in a world without foundational truths as grounds for choice. Religions, in contrast, depend on such grounding. They determine what we ought to do by appealing in the last instance to the will of God, as revealed to priests or prophets. The will of God is in this sense taken as universal and ultimate, a pure and absolute reality beyond which human enquiry cannot hope to go. Secular beliefs might well find another ultimate reality to occupy the same structural position of authority: reason, for example, or the moral law, or perhaps the laws of nature. Such metaphysical values are taken as the ultimate foundations on which all other values depend.

But if values are shaped by language, and language divides the world differently from culture to culture, there can be no appeal to a universal, grounding reality. The will of God might or might not exist but, as history has shown, it seems in practice to be a site of considerable struggle, since both sides in a conflict commonly claim it for their cause. Something similar goes for reason and nature. They are often cited, in the event, as supporting opposite points of view: right and left, feminist and anti-feminist, queer and homophobic, white supremacist and anti-racist.

Can there be, then, an ethics of deconstruction, an ethics without metaphysics? Derrida's own work is sceptical and yet, he insists, 'affirmative'. On the one hand, the element of the other in the selfsame—the difference within cultures, languages, subjects—undermines both totalitarianism and nationalism, as well as all other attempts to bring societies or groups into line with a single identity. On the other hand, Derrida argues, it does not do away with the responsibility to take account of the existing differences.

Values not only have a history; they also differ from themselves. They can therefore be modified, if not in the light of a fixed idea of the good, at least in the hope of realizing, one day, the trace of an alternative that also informs them. Derrida calls this way of thinking 'messianicity': not the promise of a specific messiah, who would fulfil an individual scripture, Christian, say, or Jewish, but the expectation of a different future 'to come' (*avenir à venir*).

Heroism

Deconstruction, then, assumes that we make moral and political choices. Could there be an ethics of psychoanalysis? In Lacan's view, since neurosis follows from repression, and neurosis is destructive, it follows that we should never give up on our desire. This proposition, it turns out, is neither as simple nor as hedonistic as it sounds. It certainly does not legitimate helping yourself to whatever you (think you) want, because desire is unconscious, and the object of our conscious wishes may well be only a stand-in for something unrecognized, however much we seem consciously to want that, and only that.

According to Lacan, the first object is always lost to the subject. The initial object of the libido in Freud is the mother. For Lacan, however, the Mother (capital M) is not a person, but a structural position, always lost to the subject who enters the order of language and culture by submitting to the paternal *Non/Nom*. Substitutes for the lost object beckon with the promise of immeasurable enjoyment, but do not deliver perfect gratification. Lacan perceives heroism as the pursuit of the lost object— whatever the cost.

His example in *The Ethics of Psychoanalysis*, the *Seminar* of 1959–60, is Antigone. Lacan dismisses the view that satisfaction comes from 'the goods' of duty, self-denial, serving the interests of others. The superego, or conscience, is exorbitant: it simply increases its demands. He has no time for good sense, as orthodoxy understands that term. Antigone, too, neglects the goods. King Creon has decreed that the corpse of her brother, the traitor Polynices, should remain unburied as an example to others. Antigone, without extenuating the treason, is driven to give Polynices proper burial, simply because he was her kin, because they shared a womb. In defiance of the law, the rules of good conduct, her obligations to her sister, the promise of happiness with her future husband, and, above all, good sense as others perceive it, she buries her brother, knowing that the penalty is to be walled up in her own tomb.

Like Freud, Lacan traces to the protagonist of a Greek tragedy his account of a drive that impels human beings beyond their conscious hopes and wishes. Lacan stresses the contradictory character of the compulsions that motivate us. Love of the lost object and the death drive are inextricably entwined with one another in desire. Antigone never gives up on hers. And although Lacan is often accused of misogyny, his heroic example is a woman.

Lacan's heroine had already been invested with mythic status in French culture. Jean Anouilh's influential *Antigone*, first performed in occupied Paris in 1944, was widely understood at the time as a debate about the merits of resistance—and the Resistance. Lacan unfolded his less ambivalent, but equally complex, reading of the Sophoclean original 15 years later.

The same *Seminar* of 1959–60 refers repeatedly to weapons of mass destruction as a threat to humankind, and can be read as offering a theoretical account of the conflicting compulsions that would prevent and incite their use: love on the one hand and, on the other, the death drive projected outwards as hate. Elsewhere in the world, this was a time of vigorous activity to counter the equally vigorous human impulse towards destruction. The British Campaign for Nuclear Disarmament was set up in 1958, with Bertrand Russell as its first president.

Sublimation

Mercifully, desire does not always require as much of us as it does of Antigone. Freud attributed the existence of civilization to the process of sublimation, which transformed raw drives into socially approved activities: artistic creation, for example. Lacan sees works of art as acknowledging the void left by the lost object when they encircle emptiness, fencing it off with a decorative surface. But sublimation is not only for artists. In most lives, Lacan believes, the drive is brought to serve the interests of civilization, taking the innocent form of making things.

Dissension

Meanwhile, Jean-François Lyotard makes the case for more contention. Unconscious desire impels us all in the form of a radical discontent, a dissatisfaction with things as we find them, a restlessness that can find one outlet among others in a commitment to social and political change. And what we need if things are to get better, Lyotard argues in *The Postmodern Condition*, is more dissension.

Consensus promotes a bland centrism, appoints the compromise candidate that no one really wants, satisfies nobody, and leaves things much as they are. Conversely, intellectual difference, inventiveness, lateral thinking, heterogeneity all promote modifications of the existing rules and conventions. Dissension disrupts the status quo and scatters convention to the winds.

It is worth remembering that some of these views were first formulated when totalitarianism in the Soviet Union promoted self-congratulation in the West. The main political dangers were perceived as totality on the one hand and complacency on the other. In a later context, poststructuralist analyses have a different bearing on the self-evident divisions issuing from identity politics,

Consensus

Q. Surely we need more consensus, not less? Haven't Western democracies set as their goal the kind of discussion that would resolve conflict and allow people of differing convictions to live in harmony?

A. Yes, if consensus centres on remedying injustices. But tolerance slides easily towards indifference. People turn a blind eye to wrongs as the efficiency of the economy becomes the only shared commitment. Similarly, compromise turns readily into conservatism, when the familiar seems safer than the unknown. 'Neutrality', it often turns out, is not neutral at all, but sides with the way things are to avoid the dissension that might lead to change for the better. A refusal to hear unpopular opinions may leave them uncontested. Consensus, then, may come into conflict with reform.

local and national. Memo to admirers of Donald J. Trump, Boris Johnson, and others: it's good to have outlaws who challenge authority but it's not always good to put them in charge.

Language games

How in any period is dissension to be actively fostered as disagreement that stops short of violence? And where does the opportunity to construct and debate different views find its theoretical place within a poststructuralist account of human culture? Or what in the nature of signifying practice releases inventiveness and heterogeneity?

In answer, Lyotard turns to Ludwig Wittgenstein's account of language as a series of 'games'. Utterances can be divided into various types, which depend on shared rules, and produce a relationship between the speakers, just as games require rules and generate a relationship between players.

For instance, Lyotard explains, a statement of 'fact' places the speaker in the position of someone who knows, and the addressee as someone who agrees or disagrees. By contrast, a question reverses the roles: if I ask the way, I attribute knowledge to my interlocutor. If I give an instruction, I lay claim to authority. The person I address can either accept the proffered position, or refuse it and dissent, mislead, or disobey. In all these instances, the speaker implicitly either claims or cedes power, while the addressee may either take up or withhold the subject-position on offer. We can never predict with certainty the 'move' our interlocutor will make.

In this sense, then, Lyotard says, dialogue can be seen as a succession of manoeuvres, and 'to speak is to fight, in the sense of playing', although he hastens to add that we do not always play to win. There is also a pleasure to be gained from sheer linguistic creativity: telling jokes, recounting stories, producing slogans, making puns. Perhaps in these instances, our opponent is conventional language itself.

Lewis Carroll's Humpty Dumpty would surely have agreed. He conducts the entire conversation with Alice as a series of moves. At one point he demands to return to the last remark but one. Not surprisingly, Alice cannot remember what it was. '"In that case we may start afresh," said Humpty Dumpty, "and it's my turn to choose a subject—" ("He talks about it just as if it was a game!" thought Alice).' It is no accident that *Through the Looking Glass*, which consistently challenges the reader, as well as Alice, with riddles and linguistic conundrums, is structured as a chess game.

In everyday exchanges language games need not be a matter of conscious intention. Lyotard's account is designed to describe what takes place, whether the speakers concerned know it or not. But the process could become conscious. By winning a round, replying unexpectedly, altering the terms of the debate, or dissenting from the dominant position, we can shift the power relations, however imperceptibly.

Jean-François Lyotard, 1924–98

The book that brought Lyotard to international—and controversial—attention was *The Postmodern Condition: A Report on Knowledge* (1979, English translation 1984), which defined the postmodern as 'incredulity toward metanarratives'. Lyotard's metanarratives, or 'grand narratives', are those totalizing accounts of the world that offer to explain everything, including 'little narratives', the familiar stories that represent our own culture to us.

Little stories—individual records, fictions, histories of particular moments—identify heroes and villains, and name the knowledges worth possessing. They confirm shared meanings and values. At the same time, the values inscribed in these little stories are often incommensurable with one another, demonstrating that culture is not homogeneous or uniform.

Grand narratives, by contrast, reduce the little stories to their own terms. Indeed, they reduce all history to a single trajectory: the progressive emergence of rational values, for instance, or 'development' towards the global market. The inevitable triumph of the working class was just such a metanarrative, and *The Postmodern Condition* has not been popular with Marxists.

The Differend (1983) argues that disputes between incommensurable positions cannot be resolved without injustice to one side or the other.

Nodal points

Powerless though we might seem to be, everyone is located, Lyotard points out, in circuits of communication; we all occupy 'nodal points' where messages are received and retransmitted. Interference with the message, however slight, changes the content, or the place of the addressee, and has the capacity to alter in the process the power relations it was designed to reaffirm.

Such modifications, as we know, take place all the time. You pass on an instruction, but reduce the urgency. The management demands a report on the low sales figures, and your response unexpectedly implicates their own negligence. At times of war, each side redefines the other's message: a 'war on terror' becomes a 'war against Islam', and in the process constitutes a rallying call to East against West.

Fiction can invite a shift of sympathy, and so of allegiance. In *Wide Sargasso Sea* Jean Rhys retells the story of Mr Rochester's mad wife from Bertha Mason's own point of view. When Baz Luhrmann moves the setting of *William Shakespeare's Romeo + Juliet* from Renaissance Verona to Verona Beach, CA, he turns a play about the conflict between romance and arranged marriage into the depiction of a high-tech, high-expenditure society that crushes innocence.

Creativity

Gilles Deleuze shares Lyotard's commitment to inventiveness. Creativity in all spheres, including art, science, and philosophy, is a mode of resistance, he argues. Deleuze draws on poststructuralism, while standing outside its concern with the signifier. Instead, he sees language merely as a way of policing thought, a system of instructions, the symbolic *order*. The rules of traditional philosophical exchange, too, inhibit freedom of speech, while psychoanalysis is nothing more than an effort to bring desire under control and into line.

Deleuze repudiates systems, codes, regulations. Instead, desire itself is revolutionary: it always wants *more*, beyond the reach of language. 'What we look for in a book', for instance, 'is the way it transmits something that resists coding.' Since desire does not define its object beforehand, creativity requires experimentation without predetermined objectives.

Advances are fostered, Deleuze maintains, by deterritorialization. Historical change deterritorializes, uproots populations, continuously reassigning territories between groups, nations, states. Where territories delimit and constrain peoples and cultures, revolutions intensify the process of change, opening up new spaces. The imperative is to cross frontiers, take flight. And this goes for thought too. Cultural deterritorialization permits new art forms, discoveries, ways to think.

Gilles Deleuze, 1925–95

Radical French philosopher, admirer of Spinoza, Nietzsche, and Foucault, who also wrote on the novel, poetry, and film. Deleuze made his name with *Difference and Repetition* (1968). He valued multiplicity and impersonality over identity and replaced the subject with *assemblages*, historical, collective, and in flux. Writing with Félix Guattari in *Anti-Oedipus* (1972), he rejected psychoanalysis as systematizing and institutionalized. Where desire is impersonal, active, and revolutionary, psychoanalysis confines it to the subject and reduces it to the effect of an Oedipal lack. The history of philosophy is the discipline's own version of the Oedipus complex, he argued, negative and exclusionary, while in cinema and writing authorial explanations similarly castrate the work of art. Art has a special role in challenging the established order and (some) Anglo-American fiction, in particular, resists the rules, inventing new options in the process.

Dissent

The avant-garde

'Art is resistance,' claims Deleuze, rhetorically. 'It resists death, slavery, infamy, shame.' Many of his chosen authors and *auteurs* represent the modernist revolt against realism. In an explicitly polemical essay, 'Answering the Question: What is Postmodernism?', Lyotard, too, puts forward a strong plea for artistic dissent. Cultures, he argues, need the challenge of new forms if they are not to settle into complacency or, worse, the terror that is totalitarianism.

But, from his perspective, art is not always resistance. Lyotard's target in the essay is what he calls realism. Realism, he claims, confirms the illusion that we are able to seize hold of reality, truth, the way things 'really' are. Photography, film, and television, offering themselves as windows on 'the facts', complete the programme of ordering visual space in accordance with truth that began with Renaissance painting.

In 15th-century Italy, painters began to depict the world in obedience to the rules of fixed-point perspective. As long as all the lines understood to be parallel to the ground converged at a single vanishing point in the picture, and as long as objects were diminished and foreshortened accordingly, three dimensions were miraculously inscribed on a two-dimensional canvas, and the 'truth' appeared in painting. But this 'truth' masked its dependence on geometry; it was an illusion. On condition that the viewer stood in exactly the right position, opposite the vanishing point, and at the distance, scaled for size, of the painter from the scene, and as long as the picture was viewed with one eye closed, the illusion of truth was conjured out of a very skilful fiction.

Seventeenth-century Dutch realism rendered the world we believe we know with an exceptional level of accuracy. In 1658 Pieter de Hooch shows space receding in and beyond a courtyard in Delft (see Figure 8). He also includes in this domestic setting three

8. Pieter de Hooch's three-dimensional space encloses women.

figures that realism places as belonging there, all of them female. Under the arch, one woman looks outwards through the open door but does not venture forth.

Realism, Lyotard argues, protects viewers from doubt. It comforts us with a picture of the world we seem to know and, in the process, confirms our own status as knowing subjects by reaffirming that picture as true. Things are, human beings are, and, above all, we are just as we have always supposed.

'Postmodernity', in Lyotard's account, names a different literary and artistic mode, rather than a particular period. Duchamp's challenge to realism is intelligible as postmodern. 'You want realism?' Richard Mutt's urinal seemed to ask. 'I'll give you reality itself, a readymade urinal, exactly the kind you see every day.' Er, that is, the kind men see every day. Well, Western men, anyway. Reality itself, when you come to think of it, is also culturally relative.

In the 20th century, experimental art and literature challenged the dominance of realism, proclaimed it the effect of a trick, and broke with its values to acknowledge the impossibility of making truth present in the signifier. One branch of the new experimentalism—Lyotard calls it modernism—devoted itself to defining in stories and artworks a nostalgia for unnattainable presence. The other, the postmodern, a component of modernism, but positive, rejoiced in the freedom its loss conferred. Postmodernism celebrates the capability of the signifier itself to create new forms and, indeed, new rules.

M. C. Escher's lithographs defy realism. Exactly three centuries after Pieter de Hooch depicted an enclosing courtyard, Escher's *Belvedere* shows a series of viewing platforms open to the elements (see Figure 9). His gazebo mimics a fairy-tale castle, complete with a dungeon. On the middle level a nobleman contemplates the mountain view, while behind his back a suitor and his servant climb up towards his daughter. The ladder is based inside the middle floor but propped outside the top one. This young woman also gazes out—or perhaps in. She has her back to the mountains, since here the illusion of three dimensions does not hold. The top floor turns out to be at right angles to the one below.

On the lowest level an artist or artisan constructs an impossible object from the diagram at his feet. The Necker cube demonstrates the optical illusion created by the representation of

9. Does Escher mock realism, or draw attention to art's power of creating illusions?

three dimensions on a flat surface. Which surface faces outwards? Escher's maker wants to have it both ways.

And so, in his own way, does Escher. The lithograph cites realism only to show the power of art to tease the viewer with a different arrangement of the visual space.

Terror

The postmodern, or the avant-garde, refuses to obey pre-existing rules. Instead, Lyotard argues, the postmodern artist and writer are working without regulations, in order to discover what the rules governing their work will have been. The postmodern is both too early and too late: too early for the public, since it must be new; too late for the author, who cannot know in advance whether it will prove to be intelligible, pleasurable, or absurd. Escher was only grudgingly recognized by the art world but embraced by popular culture. Duchamp's *Fountain* was rejected by the Independents; now authorized copies are priceless.

In this sense, the postmodern poses not only a challenge but a question. 'What do you think?', it implicitly asks. Or, better, 'Are you able to think beyond the limits of what is already acceptable? Is it possible to accommodate the previously unknown?'

Both Nazism and Stalinism deplored the avant-garde. National Socialism endorsed classicism and pronounced modern art decadent; Stalin promoted Socialist Realism at the expense of the experimental forms that had developed immediately after the Revolution. Each regime believed that it possessed the truth, and that art should reaffirm that conviction by reproducing reality as the authorities defined it.

Lyotard associates the fantasy of possessing the truth with terror. The avant-garde is not just a matter of style. Because it poses questions, it undermines all certainties, including the certainty

that you possess the truth—and are entitled to kill people in
its name.

The event

In all these instances, poststructuralism takes a radical position on
the way things are, while rejecting programmes, blueprints, and
all advance attempts to define the preferred future. In this it
respects its own scepticism concerning our access to a truth
beyond the signifier, a political certainty endowed with the power
to determine what must happen, especially in a world that does
not yet exist.

Alain Badiou breaks with poststructuralism, however, to reinstate
the idea of truth, although not in the traditional form of a
statement that corresponds with a given state of affairs. Instead,
what Badiou calls truth is summoned by an *event*, in a distinctive
version of the poststructuralist term I described in Chapter 5.

The radical event

Q. How do I distinguish between Badiou's event and, say, a Hitler
rally? National Socialism broke with the old order; it too induced
a different way to be and invited new allegiances. The question is
particularly pressing in times of popular nationalist fervour.

A. The difference lies in the naming. The radical event as Badiou
understands it is open-ended, its consequences incalculable and
undecidable. National Socialism, by contrast, defined the specific
project of taking one people under one leader towards its true
destiny. The Nazis set out to impose a future they foresaw—and
their regime led to nothing but totality and terror. Beware of
leaders who predict outcomes, not least when these involve
national sovereignty or recovered greatness.

Badiou's event is by definition unnameable in the vocabulary that is taken for granted at the time. Once it is recognized as a radical rupture, it transforms the prevailing conventions, and invites new allegiances. The event happens—the French Revolution, for instance, but also relativity theory, the birth of tragedy, or falling in love—while the subject its affirmation brings into being is open to its implications and true to the changes it brings about.

There can be no doubt about Badiou's own allegiances. He wants to reclaim the word 'communism'—not for what he calls the 'despotic grey totality' of the old USSR, but as the release of multiplicity in an insurrection against the state's support for unjust and unprincipled capitalism. But he is adamant that it is not philosophy's job to prescribe political action. Althusser was wrong, he maintains, to suppose that philosophy was a political practice. Instead, there are four domains of practice: politics, science, art, and love. Events take place in those domains and philosophy's task is to make sense of what happens there, to welcome events into thought.

Alain Badiou, 1937–

Philosopher who worked—and disputed—with Foucault, Lyotard, and Deleuze. Post-Marxist, Badiou is arguably also post-poststructuralist, drawing on the insights of Lacan and Althusser but refusing to see the subject as given by language, or language as limiting the possibilities of thought. He developed his position in *Being and Event* (1988) and has written copiously since then, including brief but astute commentaries in *A Pocket Pantheon* on some of the theorists discussed in this book. In 2009 he co-organized a conference in London on *The Idea of Communism*. A stylist, even in translation, he holds that philosophy should be appealing, as well as intelligible.

Fiction

If truth is not grounded in a reality beyond itself, if it is not discernible outside the event, if our understanding of what's possible is bounded by culture, how can we speculate on the present and the future? Badiou, a novelist and playwright himself, answers, 'in fiction'. Fiction makes no truth claims but puts forward hypotheses about what exists, what constitutes heroism, what ought to be done. Poststructuralism allots a special place to fiction in Lacan's reading of *Antigone*, Barthes's interpretation of Balzac's *Sarrasine*, and Deleuze's attention to Herman Melville, Franz Kafka, and Jack Kerouac. Derrida tells a love story in *The Post Card*.

What is the appropriate genre for fiction now? There can be no rules in advance, of course, but only new forms, or old forms reappropriated for new purposes. In 'A Postmodern Fable' Lyotard radically reinvents one of the oldest genres of all. Fables are conventionally explanatory and consoling. Aesop's, for example, show how things came to be as they are, or disseminate customary morality. Fables provide answers to real questions, while remaining by definition fictitious: they 'fabulate'.

By contrast, Lyotard's postmodern instance of the genre does not offer much consolation; it provides no answers but poses a question; it fabulates very little, but reproduces the conclusions of modern science. And it begins at the end of the story:

> 'What a Human and his/her Brain—or rather the Brain and its Human—would resemble at the moment when they leave the planet forever, before its destruction; that, the story does not tell.'
> So ends the fable we are about to hear.
> The Sun is going to explode.

'A Postmodern Fable' asks whether 'we' can survive the inevitable explosion of the sun four and a half billion solar years from now.

All stars eventually extinguish themselves in a conflagration, and the sun is no exception. It will go up in flames, taking the earth with it. Will human beings escape?

Since 1992 when the story was first published, awareness of the climate emergency has made the question much more pressing: we may not, after all, have four and a half billion years to come up with an answer. But a happy ending may well presuppose that 'we' become something other than we are, beings capable of survival in circumstances quite different from those we evolved in.

What are 'we'? Lyotard's fable replies that human beings are an effect of 'the fortuitous conjugation of various forms of energy', the molecular composition of the earth's surface in conjunction with solar radiation, which led to the formation of living cells. There followed cell division, a form of birth and death, then sexual reproduction, natural selection, language... The postmodern fable thus explains the origins of things, after all. Its protagonist, however, is not a living being, which is no more than an accidental effect, but energy itself.

According to Lyotard's futuristic fable, scientific resources were increasingly devoted to human survival beyond the end of the world. The human body, adapted to life on earth, would need prosthetic remodelling or replacement in such a way that the brain would continue to work in a different environment. But what it would be like the story does not say.

Since this is a postmodern fable, the text includes its own commentary on the story it tells. The fable, it points out, does not repudiate realism: on the contrary, it embraces information about the world that is scientifically verifiable. But it is not science. Instead, as fiction, it represents a special organization of language, which is itself a form of energy in a particularly complex state. Fiction involves imagination. Science and technology also involve imagination—to a high degree—but they are subject in the end to the criteria of truth: they submit their propositions to the test of verification or falsification.

Fables don't. They are entitled to leave the answers in suspense, releasing in the process the options for invention, discovery, lateral thinking on the part of the reader. We are invited to supply the ending we would like—and in the process to suppose ourselves superseded by something barely imaginable.

What makes this fable postmodern, Lyotard argues, is its repudiation of the teleological structure of the grand narratives that characterize modernity. 'Modernity' begins, in this instance, with Christianity, which offers an archetypal grand narrative. According to the Christian account, the end of the world will reinstate the condition that was there at the beginning. The reign of God, in other words, will restore the relationship with human beings as it existed before the Fall. During the Enlightenment, secular grand narratives rewrote this story, promising for the benefit of human beings the restoration of the reign of nature, or the classless society, the original state of affairs before things went wrong.

Lyotard's postmodern fable has no place for the assumption that history is motivated by a design that works in the end for the good of the human subject. On the contrary, the fable treats time as a series of discontinuous states of energy, and the subject as a temporary effect, not a motive but an incidental by-product of a transitory condition of matter.

The fable is bleak, then, as befits a story told in line with postmodern uncertainty, the condition theorized by poststructuralism itself. But it is not pessimistic, since it leaves the future open. The Brain and its Human are not at the mercy, it indicates, of a malignant force, any more than we are the creation of a benevolent designer. Instead, what is to become of us is to some degree up to us. The end of the story remains, then, to be decided. Moreover, the tale is not a prediction but a fabulation. It asks, Lyotard says, 'not that it be believed, but that we reflect on it'.

Poststructuralism and reflection

What poststructuralism offers is, in the end, an opportunity and a cause for reflection. It proposes a lexicon and a syntax, which is to say a vocabulary and an indication of the ways words legitimately relate to each other. But the language poststructuralism puts forward—on the basis, of course, in the first instance, of a study of language itself—is more useful in promoting the uncertainty of questions than in delivering the finality of answers.

The project is that the questions might replace the bewildering alternatives of the intellectual market-place with a more sharply focused undecidability that specifies the options, while leaving them open to debate. In that respect, in its emphasis on the degree to which we make our own story, subject to certain specifiable constraints, poststructuralism is at once sceptical towards inherited authority and affirmative about future possibilities. Above all, it asks, like Lyotard's fable, that we reflect on it.

Common concerns

It is openness to an undetermined future that constitutes the common thread linking the various views I have considered. Dissent is not only a prescription for change. It also prevails among poststructuralist positions and theories that not only overlap but also conflict. Each of the theorists I have discussed here finds a distinct focus, or offers to advance our understanding in a fresh way; they frequently disagree among themselves.

Derrida makes his own differences particularly explicit. He is deeply critical of what he sees as binary oppositions in the work of

Foucault and Lacan. And yet, when he names those with whom he feels the closest affinity, he includes Foucault and Lacan, as well as Althusser, Deleuze, and Lyotard. Foucault, he concedes,

> seems to me more of a 'deconstructor' than Lévi-Strauss, to the
> extent that he was more impatient and more rebellious, less
> politically conservative and more engaged in 'subversive' actions
> and 'ideological' struggles…But from another point of view, it
> seems to me that Lacan was more daring as a 'deconstructor' than
> Foucault. I have therefore felt—and still feel today—closer to Lacan
> than to Foucault.

As Derrida's vocabulary here indicates ('impatient', 'rebellious', 'daring'), what he sees as shared is opposition to the currency of traditional theoretical exchange.

Derrida's own point of defiance is differance (with an *a*), not a thing, neither a word nor a concept, and yet the only source of meaning. Itself ungrounded, differance withholds the grounds for relying on what is taken for the signified truth. In defence of class struggle, Althusser made a bid for a Marxist science that would confute ideology but could not with integrity sustain the distinction. For Foucault, bodies refuse their own subjection, while resistance forms the inevitable corollary of power. In *S/Z* Barthes gestures towards the writable text that, while it does not exist in any kind of totality, aspires to escape from the 'parsimonious plural' of realism. Deleuze reaches for the outside of language as a place of creativity, while Badiou seeks the moment of rupture, the event that redefines everything. Lyotard's dissension affirms the value of lateral thinking, while his elisions shade into Lacan's real as an obstacle to the Cartesian *cogito*.

Poststructuralism wins some and loses some. While there is regret for what evades the signifier, and the mastery it fails to deliver, the space this failure releases offers the possibility of thinking differently. Poststructuralism takes into account the lack of guaranteed fit between the world and the language that claims to represent it, confronting determinist philosophies with a difference that multiplies the options. In the absence of certainty, multiplicity cannot constitute a promise but only an aspiration, the hope of a different future to come.

Despite the obstacles, that future remains in our hands.

Glossary

Author (capital A) traditional source and 'explanation' of the text; a means of imposing limits on the proliferation of meaning

bourgeoisie class owning the forces of production in capitalism

citationality the practice of quotation, reiteration, allusion that makes signifying practices intelligible

culture the inscription in stories, rituals, customs, objects, and practices of the meanings in circulation

deconstruction analysis of the invasion of the excluded, differentiating other into the selfsame (see **trace**)

differance the deferral of the imagined concept or meaning by the **signifier**, which takes its place, relegating it beyond access; the only (but non-positive) 'origin' of meaning (Derrida)

drive the psychic representative of an instinct

event occurrence that ruptures the social fabric, initiating radical changes in political practice and vocabulary

ideology forms of social exchange justifying the dominance of the ruling class (Marx); assumptions, values, the obvious, inscribed in material practices (Althusser)

logocentrism supposition that meanings have priority over the **signifier**, that language is the expression of a prior concept existing as pure intelligibility

metanarrative (grand narrative) comprehensive, totalizing story that accounts for everything and reduces all little stories to its terms (Lyotard)

metaphysics quest for underlying realities, the ultimate foundations on which analysis can rest

Other (capital O) the **symbolic order**, which exists outside us, and is the condition of becoming a **subject** (Lacan)

phonocentrism privilege accorded to the voice, speech

presence the thing itself as actuality, idea, or meaning, directly encountered without the intervention of the **signifier**. An originary purity undifferentiated from itself, the myth that drives **metaphysics** (Derrida)

real the unnameable; that which precedes or escapes the **symbolic order**; lost organic being (Lacan)

semiology the study of signifying practice; analysis of the inscription of meanings in culture

semiotic, the sounds and rhythms that disrupt 'thetic' (rational) thematic meaning (Kristeva)

signifier sound, image, written shape, object, practice, or gesture invested with meaning

structuralism identification of universal structures underlying culture, usually as binary oppositions; belief that human beings are the effect of structures that escape their awareness

subject that which is capable of signifying practice and thus agency, choice; at the same time, the effect of subjection to the **symbolic order**

symbolic order the discipline which is the condition of the ability to symbolize or signify; the order of language and **culture** (Lacan)

trace the residue in the **signifier** of the excluded, differentiating term, and so a source of its meaning (Derrida)

transcendental signified the (imagined) founding meaning that would hold all other meanings in place (see **metaphysics**)

References

Chapter 1: Creatures of difference

The most useful translation of Ferdinand de Saussure's *Course in General Linguistics* is by Wade Baskin (London: Fontana, 1974). (The Roy Harris translation does not use the vocabulary poststructuralism was to take up, and so fails to indicate how influential the book was to be.) The crucial points are made in the chapter on 'Linguistic Value' (Part 2, chapter 4). Julia Kristeva explains the semiotic in her *Revolution in Poetic Language* (New York: Columbia University Press, 1984), pp. 19–106. 'The Death of the Author' was first published in English in 1967 and did not appear in French until 1968. It is included in Roland Barthes, *Image-Music-Text* (London: Fontana, 1977), pp. 142–8.

Chapter 2: Difference and culture

For 'Soap Powders and Detergents' see Roland Barthes, *Mythologies* (London: Vintage, 2009), pp. 31–3. Skincare is discussed in the subsequent collection, *The Eiffel Tower and Other Mythologies* (Berkeley: University of California Press, 1997), pp. 47–9. Saussure defines semiology in the *Course* (Introduction, chapter 3). Karl Marx and Friedrich Engels, *The German Ideology* is available in several editions. The most useful passages are also reproduced in David McLellan, ed., *Karl Marx: Selected Writings* (Oxford: Oxford University Press, 1977). Louis Althusser's essay, 'Ideology and Ideological State Apparatuses (Notes Towards an Investigation)' appears in his *Lenin and Philosophy and Other Essays* (London: New Left Books, 1971), pp. 121–73. Roland

Barthes discusses the in-difference of structuralism in his *S/Z* (London: Jonathan Cape, 1975), p. 3.

Chapter 3: The differed subject

The hermaphrodite's story is told in Michel Foucault, ed., *Herculine Barbin* (New York: Pantheon, 1980). For an account of bio-power, see *The History of Sexuality, Volume 1: An Introduction* (London: Allen Lane, 1979), pp. 133–59. Lacan's comments on the symbolic order as the Other, embodied in the No/Name of the Father, as well as the lack that impels desire, recur at intervals in the course of his work. Some of the references are collected in Dylan Evans, *An Introductory Dictionary of Lacanian Psychoanalysis* (London: Routledge, 1996). For the conflict between 'the goods' and desire, see especially Jacques Lacan, *The Ethics of Psychoanalysis* (London: Routledge, 1992), pp. 311–25. Lacan argues that there is no perfect sexual relation in *On Feminine Sexuality: The Limits of Love and Knowledge* (New York: W. W. Norton, 1998), esp. p. 17. Julia Kristeva's comments on our own inevitable foreignness are from her *Strangers to Ourselves* (New York: Columbia University Press, 1991), pp. 189, 191. René Descartes defines the *cogito* in his *Discourse on Method* (Harmondsworth: Penguin, 1968), pp. 53–4.

Chapter 4: Difference or truth?

Jacques Derrida deconstructs Lévi-Strauss in 'The Violence of the Letter', *Of Grammatology* (Baltimore: Johns Hopkins University Press, 2016), pp. 109–52. The account of Saussure and differance precedes this (pp. 29–79). The most reliable translation of the essay on 'Differance' is David B. Allison's in Jacques Derrida, *'Speech and Phenomena' and Other Essays on Husserl's Theory of Signs* (Evanston, Ill.: Northwestern University Press, 1973), 129–60. For Thierry de Duve's account of the implications of *Fountain*, see *Kant after Duchamp* (Cambridge, Mass.: October, 1999).

Chapter 5: Difference in the world

Derrida dismisses the *hors-texte* in '…That Dangerous Supplement…', *Of Grammatology*, 153–78, pp. 172 and 177. For 'de-presentation', see p. 220. He names the desire for presence on pp. 155–6. For the record of the Glasgow conference, see Nigel Fabb, Derek Attridge, Alan Durant, and Colin MacCabe, eds, *The Linguistics of Writing: Arguments between Language and Literature* (Manchester: Manchester University Press, 1987), 252–64, p. 260. Bruno Latour draws on poststructuralism to point out the implications of climate change in *Down to Earth: Politics in the New Climatic Regime* (Cambridge: Polity, 2018). I have quoted Jean-François Lyotard, *The Differend* (Manchester: Manchester University Press, 1988), p. 57. For quotations from Sarah Kofman, see her *Smothered Words* (Evanston, Ill.: Northwestern University Press, 1998), pp. 7 and 34. Derrida states that what happened in the holocaust 'remains without a name and without a concept' in *For What Tomorrow* (Stanford, Calif.: Stanford University Press, 2004), p. 138. He suggests we should attend to primates in *For What Tomorrow*, pp. 36 and 43. On animal emotions, see Karsten Brensing, *What Do Animals Think and Feel?* (London: Head of Zeus, 2019). The cucumber experiment is described on p. 152. The laughing orang-utan is at <https://www.youtube.com/watch?v=rNWPqfCJDnc>. Derrida regrets the loss of Lyotard in *The Work of Mourning* (Chicago: University of Chicago Press, 2001), p. 214. I have slightly modified the translation of Barthes's observations on love in *A Lover's Discourse: Fragments* (London: Vintage, 2002), pp. 20–1 and the interpolations are mine. Deleuze's 'He Stuttered' appears in his *Essays Critical and Clinical* (London: Verso, 1998), pp. 107–14. I have also quoted p. 55.

Chapter 6: Dissent

Lacan reads *Antigone* in *The Ethics of Psychoanalysis* (London: Routledge, 1992), pp. 241–87. Lyotard's theory of dialogue as conflict appears in *The Postmodern Condition: A Report on Knowledge* (Manchester: Manchester University Press, 1984), pp. 10, 15. 'Answering the Question: What is Postmodernism?' is appended to the same volume. I have quoted Gilles Deleuze from *Negotiations, 1972–90* (New York: Columbia University Press, 1995), pp. 22, 174. Alain Badiou discusses the danger of naming the event in *Ethics: An Essay on the Understanding of Evil* (London: Verso, 2001), pp. 72–7 and *Infinite Thought* (London: Continuum, 2003), p. 167. I have quoted *Infinite Thought*, p. 127. For Badiou's proposition that philosophy should charm, see 'French: Language Stripped Bare by its Philosophers', *Dictionary of Untranslatables*, ed. Barbara Cassin (Princeton: Princeton University Press, 2014). Badiou names fiction as the support for commitment in *Philosophy for Militants* (London: Verso, 2012), pp. 77–80. The fable is one of Lyotard's *Postmodern Fables* (Minneapolis: University of Minnesota Press, 1997), pp. 83–101. Derrida names his affinities in *For What Tomorrow*, pp. 6, 11.

Further reading

Work on cultural diversity and translation often supports the
poststructuralist account of language, although without necessarily
pointing to any overlap. For a richly illustrated instance, see
Dennis Duncan, Stephen Harrison, Katrin Kohl, and Matthew
Reynolds, *Babel: Adventures in Translation* (Oxford: Bodleian
Library, 2019). Daniel Everett tells a fascinating story of linguistic
and cultural difference in *Don't Sleep, There are Snakes* (London:
Profile, 2008).

Introductions to theory, including mine, necessarily simplify the
issues, in some cases to the point where they are barely recognizable.
Among those that don't, and from a literary-critical point of
view, Andrew Bennett and Nicholas Royle offer a lively alternative
to the usual summaries and digests in *An Introduction to
Literature, Criticism and Theory* (London: Routledge, 2016). As
far as specific authors are concerned, Malcolm Bowie can be
trusted in *Lacan* (London: Fontana, 1991). For a creative reading
of Derrida that foregrounds what is uncanny in his work, and
including '…That Dangerous Supplement…', see Nicholas Royle,
Jacques Derrida (London: Routledge, 2003). Simon Malpas,
Jean-François Lyotard (London: Routledge, 2003) is both clear
and scrupulous. I have given some of the issues more detailed
consideration in *Culture and the Real* (London: Routledge, 2005)
and *Criticism* (London: Profile, 2016).

By far the best way to find out more about poststructuralism, however,
is to read the texts themselves. Some (but by no means all) of these
are difficult at first, but it gets easier—like learning a language.
Roland Barthes's *Mythologies* (London: Vintage, 2009) is a
pleasure to read, and so is his *A Lover's Discourse: Fragments*

(London: Vintage, 2002). Michel Foucault's most widely influential
works are not particularly obscure: try *The History of Sexuality,
Volume 1: An Introduction* (London: Allen Lane, 1979) and
Discipline and Punish (Harmondsworth: Penguin, 1979).

Derrida's *Monolingualism of the Other; or, The Prosthesis of Origin*
(Stanford, Calif.: Stanford University Press, 1998) is approachable,
as is *Positions* (London: Athlone, 1987). *Learning to Live Finally*,
his last interview, is surprisingly outspoken (Basingstoke: Palgrave
Macmillan, 2007). Otherwise, as far as Derrida is concerned, it's a
question of what interests you. *Specters of Marx* (New York:
Routledge, 1994) argues that we can't afford to forget Marxism
(and analyses the opening scenes of *Hamlet*). In *For What
Tomorrow* (Stanford, Calif.: Stanford University Press, 2004),
a dialogue with Elisabeth Roudinesco, Derrida puts forward
relatively straightforward views on the family, anti-Semitism,
capital punishment, and other controversial issues.

As for Lyotard, *The Postmodern Explained to Children* (London:
Turnaround, 1992) sounds easier than it is. *The Inhuman*
(Cambridge: Polity, 1991) is a collection of essays, some more
polemical than others. My favourite? 'Can Thought Go On Without
a Body?' (pp. 8–23).

Deleuze is more approachable than usual on the topics of writing,
psychoanalysis, and politics in *Dialogues* (with Claire Parnet, New
York: Columbia University Press, 1987) and on cinema, Foucault,
and philosophy in *Negotiations, 1972–90* (New York: Columbia
University Press, 1995).

Badiou's *Pocket Pantheon* offers delightful comments on the work of
many of the authors I have named (London: Verso, 2009). *The
Communist Hypothesis* (London: Verso, 2010) and *Philosophy
for Militants* (London: Verso, 2012) make good reading
for—well—militants.

Index

Index

GERMAN
PHILOSOPHY
A Very Short Introduction
Andrew Bowie

German Philosophy: A Very Short Introduction discusses the idea that German philosophy forms one of the most revealing responses to the problems of 'modernity'. The rise of the modern natural sciences and the related decline of religion raises a series of questions, which recur throughout German philosophy, concerning the relationships between knowledge and faith, reason and emotion, and scientific, ethical, and artistic ways of seeing the world. There are also many significant philosophers who are generally neglected in most existing English-language treatments of German philosophy, which tend to concentrate on the canonical figures. This *Very Short Introduction* will include reference to these thinkers and suggests how they can be used to question more familiar German philosophical thought.